Praise for

MEET YOUR SOUL

"Highly recommended."

— **Dr. Wayne W. Dyer**

"One of *the* most important things that you can do is connect
with your Soul. In this heartfelt book, Elisa Romeo graciously takes
you on a profound journey to do just that."

— **Denise Linn**, best-selling author of *Sacred Space* and *Soul Coaching*®

"What I appreciate about Elisa's work is her light approach and her
depth of experience and understanding. She honors the spiritual world
without taking herself too seriously. This is a sign of a true teacher."

— **Jonas Elrod**, writer, director, and filmmaker of
In Deep Shift with Jonas Elrod and *Wake*

"*Meet Your Soul* is a wonderful book that profoundly supports the path
of honing inner guidance and discovery. Elisa shares user-friendly spiritual
practices that powerfully catalyze one's ability to decode the messages of
one's soul. If you yearn to live your life with a greater sense of wisdom and
depth, then this book will help get you there. A must read for all
those on the journey toward life mastery."

— **Katherine Woodward Thomas**, best-selling author of *Calling in "The One"*

"In this lovely book, Elisa Romeo provides clear and wise guidance to help
you come into a greater knowing of your soul. As you expand in your
capacity to see with the eyes of your soul, your life becomes increasingly
rich, magical, and filled with once-hidden meaning and purpose.
Elisa offers a pathway to discover your true magnificence."

— **Robert Schwartz**, hypnotist and author of *Your Soul's Plan*

"*Meet Your Soul* felt like coming home, looking in a mirror,
and rendezvousing with a dear friend. Elisa Romeo has created a simply
beautiful offering. *Meet Your Soul* is direct, warm, and true. For those who
are ready and willing to live from the soul, her profound yet practical
contribution through these words will be deeply felt and appreciated. How
do we uplift ourselves and others? How do we change the world? We meet
our own soul. It's really as simple and straightforward as that."

— **Annie Burnside**, author of *Soul to Soul Parenting* and *From Role to Soul*

"We're in the throes of some serious depth-privation these days, and I love how Elisa helps us pursue a deeper subjectivity. As an artist, and as a developing soul, I know it to be one of the most important endeavors in life. I'm thankful for Elisa and her work."

— **Stuart Davis**, artist and creator of *Sex, God, Rock 'n Roll*

"This book is a must read if you've been feeling stuck, feeling alone, or feeling that life is just too hard. *Meet Your Soul* not only opens your eyes to a precious sacred part of you that is limitless, wise, loving, intuitive, and immensely healing. It offers you the inspiration, guidance, and tools needed to connect you with that sacred part—your Soul. This connection changes everything: how you live your life, how you see yourself, and how you love yourself."

— **Carol Ritberger, Ph.D.**, author of *Healing Happens with Your Help*

"*Meet Your Soul* is a treasure. Guiding you into the deepest authenticity within yourself, it will help you to remember why you are meant to be here. Clear and grounded, it takes you through the building blocks you'll need to trust your inner guidance more concretely. Helping you to see, hear, and feel your beautiful soul's presence in your life, *Meet Your Soul* calls you home. This book is joyous, as a true celebration of the soul should be, and I'm thrilled to recommend it to you."

— **Gary S. Bobroff**, author of *Crop Circles, Jung, and the Reemergence of the Archetypal Feminine*

"Elisa Romeo's brave and profoundly moving book is exactly what our current generation of seekers has been looking for. Her exploration of the soul takes us beyond the usual search for spirit connection and will leave readers with a foundation for personal growth that will last long after they've turned the last page."

— **Claire Bidwell Smith**, author of *The Rules of Inheritance* and *After This*

"A charming—and gently challenging—reminder of the place of the Divine in everyday life, and a liberating illustration that we are with every breath manifesting the soul. Highly recommended."

— **Jordan Stratford**, author of *Living Gnosticism*

"*Meet Your Soul* is a beautifully crafted work. In it, Elisa Romeo offers wonderfully engaging and pragmatic guidance to overcome fear and connect to a loving source of power within. The real-life examples of 'Gremlin-Taming' Elisa offers are sure to be of service not only to those readers invested in their own personal growth, but to self-help professionals as well."

— **Rick Carson**, author of *Taming Your Gremlin*® and *A Master Class in Gremlin-Taming*®

MEET
YOUR
SOUL

MEET
YOUR
SOUL

A POWERFUL
GUIDE TO CONNECT
WITH YOUR MOST SACRED SELF

ELISA ROMEO

HAY HOUSE, INC.
Carlsbad, California • New York City
London • Sydney • Johannesburg
Vancouver • Hong Kong • New Delhi

Published and distributed in the United States by: Hay House, Inc.: www.hayhouse. com® • *Published and distributed in Australia by:* Hay House Australia Pty. Ltd.: www.hayhouse.com.au • *Published and distributed in the United Kingdom by:* Hay House UK, Ltd.: www.hayhouse.co.uk • *Published and distributed in the Republic of South Africa by:* Hay House SA (Pty.), Ltd.: www.hayhouse.co.za • *Distributed in Canada by:* Raincoast Books: www.raincoast.com • *Published in India by:* Hay House Publishers India: www.hayhouse.co.in

Cover design and interior illustrations: Jennifer Wasson of Wasson Design, www .wasson-design.com • *Interior design:* Pamela Homan

Library of Congress Cataloging-in-Publication Data

Romeo, Elisa.
  Meet your soul : a powerful guide to connect with your most sacred self / Elisa Romeo. -- 1st Edition.
    pages cm
  ISBN 978-1-4019-4342-4 (tradepaper : alk. paper)
  1. Spirituality. 2. Spiritual life. I. Title.
  BL624.R643 2015
  204--dc23

                               2014033328

Tradepaper ISBN: 978-1-4019-4342-4

10 9 8 7 6 5 4 3 2 1
1st edition, March 2015

Printed in the United States of America

To Adam.
This book is dedicated to the
courage, clarity, and fierce
Love of your Soul.
"Familiar music we meet inside,
The surrendered groom and the embodied bride."

CONTENTS

A NOTE FROM
THE AUTHOR

Throughout the book you will notice the capitalization of certain words, for example, Soul, Divine, God, and Love. *The Soul,* to me, is a specific entity that deserves honor and reverence. *The Divine,* or *God,* is not used necessarily in the religious sense but refers to the great mystery that moves us all. *Love* is an expansive, transformative energy that we can either allow to move through our systems or shut off from. All are deserving of the highlighting and respect that capitalization warrants.

Also of note is that in this book I refer to the Soul in the feminine—as "She" or "Her." Of course, not all Souls are female. If your Soul is a "He," please address Him as such.

INTRODUCTION

I wrote this book to help you become free. I realize there is potential to interpret that statement in many unflattering ways. Yet, truly, the conception of this book comes from my deepest desire for you to know yourself in a way where no thing, no one, and no event or circumstance will ever have the power to disconnect you from your Self.

As an intuitive therapist, I work with a diverse group of people: businesswomen and businessmen, individuals in jail, mothers, therapists, retired grandparents, holistic healers, and teenagers.

I have sat with individuals navigating the worst of times: callers on suicide lines—some holding guns to their heads and others who have already swallowed a bottle of pills—all desperate to understand why they have been forced to do time on this planet.

I also speak with clients living in nice homes, busy with marriage and kids. While everything is functional and looks great on the outside . . . something feels off. They feel a sense of emptiness, like the hungry presence of a hole that cannot be filled. They ask if something is wrong with them. Maybe they just need to try another hobby, change jobs, or go on a trip? They explain, "I have absolutely no reason to feel sad, depressed, or empty, especially when there is so much suffering in the world. I have it good, but something is missing . . . and I don't know what it is."

What is missing is Soul. They long for a connection with the deepest, most loving, and most knowledgeable part of themselves.

During my sessions, I merge my background as a psychotherapist with my ability to see the human energy field and meet my clients' Souls, speaking directly to them. I translate the information I get—often about health, relationships, or life purpose—and then share it with my clients.

Sometimes the information coming through is shocking, but, most often, it is not a huge surprise. Often clients sheepishly admit, "I had a feeling you were going to say that." Or, "I know that's what I should do, but I just don't know how to start." Whether surprising or expected, information from the Soul resonates. Your Soul is my boss; my job is simply to translate, confirm, and validate what you already know and feel at the deepest level of yourself.

However, what I am most passionate about is not translating but helping others *empower themselves* through knowing and hearing their own Souls' information. I help introduce my clients' ego selves to their Soul Selves and give them practical tools to help build and maintain that relationship. What I have found is that *everyone has the ability to connect directly with their Souls and the Souls of others.* And that's what you'll learn in this book.

But, really, here is my agenda: I don't just want you to meet your Soul; *I want you to fall in love with your Soul.* I want you to feel such devotion to Her that you could never put anything else or anyone else in between you and Her. In exchange for your faithfulness, She will have you fall in love with your life. Nothing gives me more joy than witnessing someone who has finally come home to her Soul.

I view disconnection from Soul as the greatest affliction of the 21st century. It distances us from a feeling relationship to the environment (resulting in the current unhealthy state of the planet); it encourages heady and detached politics; it creates separation instead of connection between people; it often manifests as disease in the body and stifles our inherent vibrancy and joy in life.

But please don't take my word for it. I want you to be an empiricist. I don't want you to merely *believe* what I am saying. I want you to run your own master experiment. If you can play and have an open mind, you can have an experience of your Soul.

When I met my own Soul, it filled a deep hole inside me, a hole I had carried for years. I had searched externally, looking to experts, programs, relationships, and philosophies for relief from my own self-contained prison. Driven by an inherent desire and intuition that freedom was somehow possible, I searched for a deep feeling of peace, acceptance, and joy, which, ultimately, I only found through my relationship to my Soul. Self-love is all about knowing the Soul. While it may be cliché, it's true: our answers truly come from within.

What I have discovered, over and over again, through thousands of sessions, is that this Soul stuff works. I have found it to be the most effective and efficient way to get true and helpful practical answers, to manifest incredible life synchronicities, and to cultivate an incredible feeling of "coming home" to yourself and to your Divine seat in the universe.

And this is what we all want deep down. In fact, many neurotically strive to feel at home through the illusionary comfort of addictions, such as eating, perfectionism, shopping, or workaholism. But none of those things will work. To come home, anytime, is simply a matter of having a direct experience of the Soul.

This guidebook to the Soul is ultimately about really deeply getting to know yourself. You meet your Soul when you begin to truly be yourself. But why is "being yourself" one of the most difficult things you'll ever do? It seems in theory as if it would be impossible *not* to do. But the reality is that we are stuffed full of complexes: other people's opinions, cultural programming, inner voices telling us to be a little "less," and the devastating effect of trauma on our ability to live up to our greatest potential. The path of standing in our authenticity can be rife with energetic battles.

This book helps you to see and win those battles. In Part, I you get a thorough explanation of what the Soul is (and isn't) so you can be clear about the mission ahead. Then, in Part II, you meet your Soul through simple inquiries, meditations, and practices. In Part III, you discover the most common blocks that arise on the path to knowing your Soul—and how to combat them. And, finally, in Part IV, you dive deep, exploring your relationship with the Soul and covering the important issues of life purpose and how to truly navigate life from a Soul perspective.

Each chapter contains some of the most powerful techniques, tools, and stories that I have come upon in my work. These have not only helped me but routinely help my clients connect to their own Souls. At times, it takes courage to hear and fight for Soul, but with the information in these pages, you will be able to do just that. Think of this book as Soul support: a lifeline to help discover, encourage, and validate your own Soul Work and Soul connection.

The only tools you will need for this journey are a journal in which to do some personal inquiries and a willingness to explore the terrain. You are about to embark on an adventure that could change everything.

Your Soul is a spiritual best friend who is always watching, waiting, and hoping that She can guide you back to your own Divinity. Not only does a relationship with the Soul allow you to live a life of connection but it is also the most *practical* relationship you will ever have. Living from Soul is the most direct and potent way to live the life you're meant to live. Your relationship to your Soul is not selfish or narcissistic; it develops the spiritual maturity and weight needed to powerfully serve the world in the unique way that only you can.

You are on purpose. You are meant to be here. The world longs for you to be your full expression. Your Soul has never left you. Your mistakes have not trapped you; instead, they serve as kindling for your authenticity. It is never too late to let go and fall into what you truly are, always will be, and always have been.

PART I

UNDERSTANDING THE SOUL

CHAPTER I

BE SOUL-CENTERED

*"The two most important days in your life are
the day you are born and the day you find out why."*
—MARK TWAIN

*"Here is a test to find whether your mission
on Earth is finished: If you're alive, it isn't."*
—RICHARD BACH

"You don't have a soul. You are a soul. You have a body."
—UNKNOWN

Most people don't spend much time thinking about the Soul. To many, it's purely a concept—the perfect topic for a heady metaphysical debate, in which we philosophize whether we do or do not "have one."

For others, Soul is a quality. A stanza of poetry, a meaningful moment, or an expressive piece of music may activate feelings of depth and reverence, and an element of the sacred; this may then be described as particularly "soulful."

Yet your Soul is not a concept or a fleeting emotion. Your Soul is a part of yourself. She is your unique representative in the universe, which longs to be in relationship to you.

The challenge to knowing the Soul is that it is not met through interpretation, analysis, and understanding from the head. The

Soul is only discovered through direct experience, feeling, and embodiment. In other words, we need to meet the Soul to know the Soul.

But why does it matter if we know our Souls?

In short, it is because your Soul is the oldest, wisest, and always-loving part of yourself, and She has access to incredible knowledge. Your Soul knows why you came to the planet, what lessons you most need to learn, and how to perfectly navigate and heal the challenges in your life. Your Soul knows exactly how to saturate your days with immense meaning, how to help you live your life's purpose, and how to achieve true success and happiness.

Your Soul sees your best, most vital self. She holds that vision when you do not. She knows what your essence wants to express here on planet Earth, and She knows it is worthy. Your Soul wants to guide you back to you—to your true identity—full in Her knowledge of who you are and why you are here. She wants you to know you were created perfectly for the mission of your life and that the most sacred gift you can give Her is to be fully you. (And the biggest gift you can give yourself is to be fully Her.)

She is the root of your consciousness. Your Soul nudges you toward your fullness, releases you from limiting beliefs, and challenges you where you withhold Love. She is the in-between of your ego self and Universal Source energy, also called the Divine or God. She is your highest God/Goddess self—you in your most authentic and genuine form. She is the incarnate of the immeasurable in your chest. She is the feeling of the incomprehensible bigness that you are. She guides you on the journey to your most authentic self—your Soul Journey.

Your Soul is Love. Yet Love from the Soul is not always gentle; at times it can leave you incredibly humbled. The Soul is fiercely "real," direct, and incredibly honest about issues you would rather look away from. The Soul is the constant daily workhorse that gives you the practical information to guide you on your life mission toward fulfillment.

When you have a direct relationship with your Soul, the benefits are life changing. I see my clients heal physical illnesses, gain confidence, create Soulful relationships, and begin to live their lives on purpose.

When you live on purpose, you live a Soul-oriented life. You live your authentic Truth and grow toward your biggest potential. You are fully alive and filled with joy and meaning.

When you are disconnected from your Soul, you are lost at sea, susceptible to the opinions and agendas of those around you. Life becomes a task to achieve, tolerate, and survive, instead of an opportunity to express your deepest heart and wildest joy.

HEARING YOUR SOUL'S ADVICE

Getting information from the Soul is not reserved for the special, unique spiritual minority. Anyone with the intention to meet his or her Soul—along with the curiosity to try—can do this. Here are just a couple of exceptional stories from my clients that show some of the real and valuable information the Soul can provide.

Jennifer is a screenwriter. She wanted to get a meeting with a big-shot producer who was seriously busy. But no matter how she tried, she couldn't get the meeting. She was working with me at the time, learning to speak with her Soul. More important, she was working on following the information she received from her Soul; she was learning to surrender to what I call the Soul's marching orders, even when they seemed confusing or irrational to her practical mind. One day, her Soul, through the imaginative process of dialoguing in her journal (covered later in this book), told her to go ice-skating that Saturday. She thought that was crazy, as ice-skating was something she would not normally do with her free time. But not only did her Soul want her to go ice-skating, She wanted her to wear her bright rainbow-striped leg warmers. Jennifer thought this was embarrassing and weird but remembered my advice of following the Soul, even when the message seems ridiculous. On Saturday she put on her leg warmers and went to the rink. Much to her surprise, the producer was there. She got on the ice and the producer skated right up to her and said, "I *love* your leg warmers!"

How did her Soul know that the producer would be there that day? How did her Soul know that the producer had a warm spot in her heart for rainbow leg warmers? The Soul has access to information our separated conscious selves do not. We need to talk directly to the Soul so we don't miss the memo.

Another client, Susan, takes care of horses. She is expected to be at the stables by 8 A.M. One morning, while dialoguing with her Soul, her Soul told her not to leave the house until 10 A.M. She thought that was ludicrous; she didn't want to get in trouble or make the horses wait for her. So she left the house and got in her car. While she was driving to the stables, a mild rainstorm turned into a flash flood. Susan was lucky to make it home. While staring out the window contemplating the crazy weather, she realized that precisely at 10 A.M. the storm "magically cleared. The sun came out dramatically. The weather change was shocking." She journaled with her Soul and got a major "I told you so." Her Soul had orchestrated this lesson so that Susan would learn to really trust and honor her Soul's guidance.

MY OWN STORY

Meeting my own Soul was one of the most dramatic experiences of my life. It happened when I was a student at Pacifica Graduate Institute, studying to become a psychotherapist. It was lunchtime, and I had a blinding headache. My friend and fellow student, Dante, a skilled masseur, saw my pain and offered to give me a massage. We rested on the thick green lawn amid other students milling about, and he began to massage my head and neck. Instantly I entered a trancelike state. I didn't want to surrender to this feeling, to let go and enter an altered reality, especially in front of other students, but I couldn't fight it, and I sank into a calm, blissful state, allowing myself to relax and enjoy the experience.

My head felt as if it was being moved in slow, small, rhythmic circles. I saw bright flashing lights. Dante noticed I was entering into a trance state and led me inside to a private room away from the other students.

In the room, my eyes fluttered, and I saw rapid and vivid visual pictures. Suddenly, without warning, my consciousness—the part of me that thinks and knows who I am—flew out of my body and hovered over my physical self. I stared with wonder at the creases in my face and the lines on my eyelids. I watched my chest contract and expand. I saw the turquoise T-shirt I was wearing, except I wasn't seeing it from my eyes, but rather from two feet above my body.

And then I had the epiphany that changed my life forever. *I am not my body.*

I had always desperately hoped that I would survive as a spirit after my physical body died, but I never completely trusted this to be true. I feared I might simply cease to exist and, like many others, felt the existential terror of disappearing into a black void.

A moment later, I met my Soul. I felt an incredible loving Presence behind me, and it was pulling me toward Her like a magnetic force. The experience was like nothing else I had ever felt; it was practically indescribable. It was the most exquisite and intelligent Love, pulsing all around and within me, welcoming me home. I joined with Her and immediately understood the struggle of the physical world. I became overwhelmed by Love and compassion, and it became clear that my priorities—my life choices—up until that point had been dictated by fear. This surprised me, as I really thought I had been courageously following my dreams. Yet in this space of unconditional Love, I suddenly understood how much fear *had* been guiding me. I had not allowed my true Self to be expressed in my current life.

I was filled with an absolute knowing that I have incarnated from the astral realm into this particular personality and lifetime to learn specific lessons—Soul Lessons—which were all planned for the purpose of my Soul's evolution. I have lived many lifetimes of different races, genders, and social standings, all for this purpose. My Soul's mission is to remind people of the reality of their own Souls' existence. In fact, I chose my particular body, my personality, and my family to assist in the process of this particular mission. I "remembered" how everyone makes the choice, from the Soul level, to be exactly who they are, complete with their talents, skills, flaws, and disabilities. Every detail is absolutely perfect for that particular person's mission, in order to strategically break them open into their unique form and flavor of Love.

It was clear from my new vantage point that all Souls have their own unique intentions, and our spiritual task as humans is to remember, to surrender, and to serve our Souls' missions, which come always from this place of Love. We do this by surrendering to and serving our Souls to the best of our abilities while we are here on Earth.

After meeting my Soul, I understood the ramifications of my addiction to the illusion of physical reality. I saw how I couldn't make room for a true and authentic connection to the Divine because of my mind's shortsighted need for "proof" in the physical world. I understood how limited my normal waking life was. Like a horse with blinders, I viewed reality through an incredibly narrow lens. How could I trust my Soul if I didn't truly believe She existed? After this meeting with Her, I could never again confuse my Self with my physical body or personality. I could now forever identify as a Soul having a human experience—not a human with a Soul.

The next few months proved to be trying. I found myself being socially awkward as my psychic abilities went into overdrive. I saw other people's Souls floating one to two feet above their heads. I also began to notice tubelike golden energy cords connecting their Souls to the centers of their hearts. I visually experienced when people spoke their truth because their spines lit up with an amazing golden energy. When they spoke from the analyzer—the preprogrammed concepts and limited ego mind in the front of their heads—the "tubes" got kinked, and the Soul energy was blocked from running smoothly through their bodies.

I slowly readjusted to society with my new sight. Instead of staring with wonder at my friends' and family's energetic bodies, I trained myself to focus on their physical bodies—like the expressions on their faces. Instead of dominating my attention, the energetic information became a rich and vibrant backstory to the living miracle of a Soul incarnated.

Once you meet your Soul, the mundane becomes miraculous and the haphazard becomes deliberate. What used to appear in your life as pointless now proves meaningful as you relax into your spiritual birthright: to be ambassador to the unique form of Love that lives within you.

CHAPTER 2

THE SPIRIT AND THE SOUL

"My life work is an attempt to ground the pure, visionary spirit in the imperfect, intoxicating sensuousness of worldly life."
—THOMAS MOORE

"In this contemporary spiritual culture of ours, we've never come near the soul. Never. We've been around the spirit but we've never been anywhere near the soul. Not at all. And it is time for us to pierce and go into the soul."
— CAROLINE MYSS

"We've spent several thousand years learning the arts of self-transcendence. But life is a matter of incarnation. The soul is an entity that lives within our human body. Over-spiritualization is a real danger. If you want to heal, you have to surrender; you have to give up control; you have to stop trying to be perfect, because eventually you have to face the fact that you cannot completely control your life."
— MARION WOODMAN

To fully understand the Soul, we must also understand the other essential parts in the experience of consciousness. The first of which is the Spirit. Though the terms *Spirit* and *Soul* are often used interchangeably, they are remarkably different things; however, they strive to work hand in hand, supporting one another.

Spirit energy is the part of us that is vast, unchanged, and associated with incredible vision, direction, and eternal oneness. Spirit is calm, clear, and collected. Spirit is full of purpose and goal oriented—unaffected by earthly drama and emotional states. Spirit motivates us to invent new ways of doing things and is the spark of cutting-edge, adventurous vision. Spirit is the holder of consciousness, the eye of awareness, and the impulse toward transcendence. Spirit is the inspired voice of unchanging certainty, which repeatedly reminds us that all elements are part of the whole, we are all interconnected, and "all is one."

On the other hand, Soul honors the realm of time, attachment, and feeling. Completely dedicated to the unique and individual paths we walk, Soul discovers Herself through the physical world and our daily practical choices. Soul calls us to embody our lives; to fully incarnate; to stay awake and open to the intense feelings this painful planet of change, illness, and ultimately death triggers in us. When we honor Soul, we become trustable, spiritually mature, and radiantly alive in the world as wisdom resonates throughout the cells of the body.

Soul is found in relationships and lures us further and deeper into our lives. She is felt in the imperfect, messy, attached places of life. Soul connects us to a sense of place and history, and warms us internally. Soul is revealed in our habits. She is felt in our daily ritual of the morning cup of coffee, consistently served in our favorite cracked pottery mug. She appears in our sacred places— the cherished bench overlooking a lake at the park or the ancient ruins that remind us of our mortality and our place in the cosmos.

She revels in and inherently trusts the body's wisdom with its complex sensory system—something the Spirit is above. But the Soul understands that our (often painful) bodily aches and symptoms hide jewels of guidance—available to be uncovered, translated, and transformed (while transforming us). We feed the Soul when we slowly sip a delicious bowl of soup, nourishing the body but also calming our relationship to the present moment.

THE ENERGIES OF SPIRIT AND SOUL

The Spirit and the Soul have seemingly opposing yet complementary energies. Soul has historically been associated with the feminine: the dark, receiving, feeling, and intuitive qualities of living. (The feminine is not limited to the narrow confines of gender or biology, but refers to the energy of the great archetypal feminine to which both men and women have access.) And Spirit often represents and is characterized as the masculine.

The feminine is represented by the "yin" energy present in the Taijitu, the Chinese yin/yang symbol. Feminine (yin) energy displays the radiance of a beautiful flower as it exposes itself, courageously dancing within the continuum of time and space. Masculine (yang) energy/Spirit holds space for the pulsing beauty of the feminine, the inherent life force within everything. The feminine is radiant, connected, and attached to this alive moment of existence, while the masculine is witness to that beauty. Sadly, like the feminine, Soul has been traditionally marginalized, minimized, and undervalued spiritually. But both are important.

We are confronted by dualities daily. We can attach ego-based morals to qualities like masculine–feminine, higher–lower, hot–cold, and pain–bliss, or we can see them as different and necessary faces of God/Goddess. The energies of Soul and Spirit together create a whole far greater than each of their parts. The polarities create universal balance and nourish and sustain each other. The masculine sun/solar consciousness shines its vision, direction, and warmth onto the earth; the feminine moon consciousness reflects the light, thus illuminating the dark. Yin is matter, the felt body, while yang is the creative energy or consciousness within that matter. Soul is based on earth; Spirit is based in light. Soul is concerned with embodiment; Spirit is preoccupied with transcendence.

In our quest for fullness, the Soul is often cast aside for the flashy and sometimes blinding vision of Spirit. The appeal of *enlightenment* has been far more popular than the Souling-down, messy process of *enlivenment*. As we reach for enlightenment, we become less attached to the shifting forms of the physical world. Through the transcendent lens of Spirit, it sometimes looks as though we are lost, confused, or regressing as we follow the necessary in-and-down spirals of the Soul Journey. But we must remember that the work of the Soul is also necessary for energetic balance. Our inner work necessitates fierce listening to the humble whisperings of the Soul. I frequently see my Spirit-identified clients harshly judge themselves for the necessary unraveling, clue seeking, and mystery honoring that occur when we bow to Soul.

But we need both Spirit and Soul. Spirit without Soul screams, *bigger, faster, more.* We can never keep up when Spirit is unchecked and unrelated. Without Soul, Spirit becomes cold, detached, and dangerously unrelated. And yet, Soul without Spirit ruminates, stagnates, and vacillates. Without Soul's acceptance of Spirit, we lose inspiration, direction, and vision. The absence of Spirit can be felt as suffocating, habitual, and stagnant.

We must become aware that these energies assist and support one another. The heart-pumping truth is that the universal and cosmic desire is for these energies to be in balance. With a tree as a metaphor, Spirit energy is represented by reaching branches—ripe with potential, searching for the sun, and striving for expansion. Soul energy works to ground, stabilize, and comfort like trusty, solid roots—all the while providing necessary life sustenance for the entire tree. They truly love one another, which is why each constantly seeks its partner, despite the obvious polarization.

SPIRITUAL ADDICTION

In her book *Conscious Femininity,* Jungian analyst Marion Woodman writes a great deal about our disconnection from Soul and our infatuation with Spirit. "Life is a matter of incarnation— the soul is an entity we have to live with in our human body. The problem is too many people in our culture try to skip over this step and go straight up into spirit."[1] She calls this crisis *overspiritualization* and notes that it often results in physical symptoms of illness or even full-blown addiction. Psychologically, this term is known as *inflation*. Like a balloon that continues to rise higher and higher into the sky, we lose orientation with the earth and the bodily way of knowing. The painful result is an inevitable crash back down, to "recover earth" through depression or illness. This is known as *deflation*. We become like Icarus in the classic Greek myth, whose wax-and-feather wings melt as he flies too close to the sun. Icarus crashes into the sea below, forced to acknowledge the limitations of physical reality and accept his mortality.

As a moth drawn to a flame, the allure of the blinding white light of Spirit can become obsessive and intoxicating. Without the Soul to integrate Spirit, we are starving and never fulfilled, searching addictively for the next high. Woodman frequently works with anorexics struggling with the hell of addiction to perfection. Anorexia is the physical embodiment of a spiritual crisis. It is the body's manifestation of the desire to avoid incarnation by rejection of heavy, feminine, and Soul-grounding weight. According to Woodman, common dream imagery for the anorexic is "white, sterile, Luciferian light." The anorexic, caught in overspiritualization, "is going for Light—she dreams everything white."[2]

Society often doesn't recognize the spiritual addict as having a problem. Spiritual teacher Adyashanti says in his book, *Emptiness Dancing*, that, as opposed to the visible signs of alcoholism or drug addiction, spiritual addiction masks itself as socially acceptable. "The seeker is told that spiritual addiction is different from all the other addictions. You're not a junkie. You're a spiritual seeker." The problem remains as long as we are fed from the illusionary highs that unbalanced Spirit provides. "This problem will last as long as there is something in you that holds out some hope for the high experience. When that begins to break down, you start to see that pleasant, wonderful, and uplifting experiences are somewhat like very pleasant and uplifting alcohol binges. They feel great for a short time and then there is an equal and opposite reaction. The spiritual high is followed by a spiritual low." Adyashanti explains that what we are truly after is freedom. "By its very nature, freedom doesn't have anything to do with sustaining a particular experience."[3]

The Soul not only has an intimate relationship with the Divine, but Her wisdom lies in the fact that She retains Her individual flavor. She does not blend or merge into a golden, hazy fog but inherently retains identity through Her own consciousness. The approachability and relationality of Soul embed Her with the necessary features of a trustworthy guide.

In fact the Soul is inherently trustable. She is the highest translator of Spirit that our ego—the other player in our consciousness—can hear. Like electrical wiring in a home, the charge needs to be grounded to avoid the buildup of static electricity. The earth is a conductor that grounds us. In the United States, electricians refer to this with the terms *ground* and *grounding,* while in the United Kingdom the equivalent terms are *earth* and *earthing.* Soul grounds us. Soul earths us. Soul does not want us to get "blown out" with a charge that would make our bodies ill.

Besides bringing us more fully into our lives, Soul connects us to the sacred in daily living. With Soul, the practical is Divine. Spirit may remind us (in a chilled-out, nonattached way) that "it's all good" and "all is one," but Soul retains Her intense individuality and attachment to Life. The Soul tenaciously, constantly, and ferociously *gives a shit.* The Soul is the victory lap of an Olympic runner, the tears shed as a lover repeatedly chooses addiction, the mother weeping and holding her dying child. The Soul is attached to the world, and Her Love contains the passion, beauty, and awe that make life worth living. The Soul wants nothing more than to encourage, witness, and celebrate the successful actualization of our Soul Lessons. She guides us to Divinity. We learn that, by embodying Soul, we play our essential, unique role in the dance of all of consciousness . . . and we know it is a goddamned honor.

It is a challenging path to consciously integrate and embody Soul. Like a mother's love for her child, living a Soul-oriented life is often complicated and confusing. It comes with no instruction manual. But it is a relationship of Love that cracks us wide open. There are tools that have helped others along their Soul Journeys, but ultimately Soul connection is about listening deep within and discovering what works for you. Soul requires inquiry, percolation, and sometimes rumination in the long and often painful birthing process. Soul invites us toward the fulfillment of our unique and particular individuation.

CHAPTER 3

THE EGO AND THE SOUL

*"The ego is who you think you are.
Our soul just is, witnessing our incarnation."*
—RAM DASS

*"We cannot go beyond the ego . . . if we have never
reached the ego. . . . We need the human ego to assimilate,
house, and channel the beyond-ego, the non-ego forces that
touch us and that we are so eager to touch in return."*
—ANN BELFORD ULANOV

"It's Britney, bitch."
—BRITNEY SPEARS

In addition to understanding the interaction between the
Spirit and the Soul, we must come to know how the Soul and the
ego work with one another to create our best lives. When I use
the term *ego,* I am referring to the part of yourself you think you
know. The ego is *who you think you are.* And because we basically
think all the time (unless we are training to not think, which we
will talk about in Chapter 8), most of our days are spent busy
identifying as *interpretations, concepts, and ideas of who we are.* Your
ego is made up of your roles (wife, mother, daughter, worker) your
identity (religion, race, gender, socioeconomic status, mental and
physical health issues), your personality (introverted/extroverted),

your temperament (generous/easily frustrated), and all the stories you have about yourself (your history and relationships). The ego lives completely in the physical, material world.

The ego relies on being seen. It wants to be recognized. It is always searching for identity. It appreciates approval. The ego is the part of you that experiences that exasperated feeling of being invisible and overlooked. If chosen last or forced to wait, the ego may angrily retort: "Do you know who I am?" Often, it gains strength and power from finding its identity based on principles of separation. "I am not that" is often as much the battle cry of the ego as "I am that." The ego looks for categories and classifications that make its specialness obvious and clear. One of my clients recently joked about her ego's incessant desire to be acknowledged: "They don't know who I think I am."

When I was in seventh grade I went to a workshop about self-esteem. We were told to write down adjectives and descriptors that described who we were. "Funny," "Italian," "loves playing tennis" were a few of the ones on my paper. I remember feeling full of the adolescent need to identify and describe who I was. I was clinging to those adjectives as though they were hopeful streams of light in an otherwise dark cavern. I wish I could have told my seventh-grade self that those words and phrases on my list of "me-ness" were ego descriptors, not reflective of the immediacy, aliveness, and feeling of who I *really* was. Those terms could not come close to satisfying the deep hunger inside me that was looking for a true experience and meeting of the "me" I was searching for.

Many people look for ego identity in their new designer clothes, their new cars, their sexual relationships, or even their identification as "mother" or "father." While these things all may point to who we are in some way, even in important ways, they will never totally replace the connection the ego needs to have with the Soul. If we leave this hole unplugged, we can desperately spend a whole lifetime in the pursuit of happiness through the next job promotion, paycheck, marriage proposal, or vacation.

THE POWER IN THE EGO

You may have seen the T-shirts or bumper stickers with the popular phrase, "Your ego is not your amigo." Some go so far as to say that E.G.O. stands for "edging God out." However, the ego does not have to be viewed as a constant spiritual pest; it actually *can* be your amigo. But only if it is seen clearly and identified as its intended spiritual cosmic purpose: a helpful separate mode of reality that allows us to experience our unique and individual lives on planet Earth for the sake of Soulful connection and unity. The ego is unbearable if it does not know its place. And *the ego's healthy place is in service and in relationship to what you truly are.* In other words, the ego's job is to help you along your Soul's path. If it is not doing this, you are living your life serving a false image of who you are. What you *truly* are at your core is the you that is behind and beyond the ego. Yes, part of you is your ego, but most of you *is not.* You are the consciousness and energy behind those roles. A healthy ego is a good assistant, the main operations manager to your Soul, the CEO of your Divine unique universe.

All of this is to say we need our egos. A healthy functioning ego is the lens (bounding us to time and space) through which the Soul sees and interacts with the world. What we need is balance and integration.

If we have too much identification with ego or too much identification with ungrounded and unintegrated Spirit, problems arise, such as inflation, spiritual narcissism, ego-identified complexes, trauma, physical ailments, or mental illness.

If we are too rooted in ego, we become densely bound to the physical appearance of things with no ability to "see through" our daily lives and glimpse a spiritual reality. An ego-heavy life results in obsession with bills, identification with accomplishments, and reliance on approval from others. There is no dance of Spirit or Soul, resulting in an inability to connect to the transcendent or a sense of purpose.

Because of this real fear of an ego-dominated life, many react with an impulsive knee-jerk reaction to destroy the ego. Yet I have worked with too many schizophrenics, caught in the hell of mental illness, surviving in a splintered ego state, to support unbridled ego annihilation. Violent, reactive ego annihilation, either through spiritual practices or through chemical substances, can, in certain circumstances, activate buried mental illness. Although drugs can at times help to open a rigid ego under certain intentional circumstances (for example, the use of Ayahuasca with a practiced guide or shaman), there are plenty of cases where dramatic LSD trips resulted in a fractured ego, which was unprepared for the intensity of the chemicalized spiritual trip. (For further reading on this topic, see the Resources section.)

Meditative practices can also lead to spirit addiction and disembodied ego imbalance. We have all had run-ins with the "not here" spiritual teachers who seem as if they are floating two feet above the ground with a zoned-out, cult-member-like look in their eyes. Our bodies do not trust this spiritual imbalance. These teachers are very different from the embodied compassion of the warm and humbled Dalai Lama or the fierce and decidedly here energy of Amma, the hugging saint. These saints have done the hard work of ego integration that true spiritual energy requires, without whiplashing into the ungrounded and all-too-common overspiritualization that prevails in the New Age collective. With the array of spiritual teaching and beliefs that bombard us constantly, navigating a spiritual life can be confusing and even potentially dangerous. By honoring ego while working with the Soul directly, you receive tailored-for-you spiritual information, sidestepping these common spiritual traps.

On its own, the ego can tell you about experiences it's had, talents it excels at, and dreams for the future, while the Soul can only show you what is necessary right now, for this moment. The ego is prerecorded; the Soul is live. That is why it's easy to understand the ego, but the Soul is a constantly changing entity, and if you want to watch the program, you have to stay tuned.

When you are in an experience of your Soul, you are the flow of life unfolding in your unique expression. You are not and can never be what you *think* you are. The world of thinking, ideas, and categorization belongs to the ego. The realm of ideas is relegated to the land of objects, symbols, and language, where classification is possible. It is important to have, essential for survival. Yet the world of experiential wisdom and discovery belongs to the Soul.

KEEPING THE EGO IN CHECK

The challenge of knowing the Soul directly is that we currently live in a culture of spiritual infancy. We are not surrounded by people who are in direct relationships with their Souls. Many religious teachers are in relationships with *ideas* or *beliefs* about who they are and why they think they are here. This is not the same thing. What it leaves in its wake is an overly intelligent, head-dominated, and wisdom-deprived culture.

It is crucial to avoid attaching to egoic beliefs about who you are. Who you truly are is an expression of the mystery living through you. It is a good practice to consistently check in: Are you, right now, allowing yourself the direct experience of your Soul? Are you living your life in accordance with what your Soul would want, or are you defended from Soul by egoic societal programming? Are you allowing your Soul to shine through your ego and imbue the planet with your unique flavor of Love? These are all necessary questions essential to our spiritual deprogramming.

The experience of discovering that you are more than your ego can actually feel to the body like destructive annihilation. The image of a sugar cube dissolving into a glass of water is a potent ego annihilation metaphor. As the ego dissolves into the greater Self, it loses its vital power. By its very nature, the ego often "fights to the death," and when we are fully identified as the ego, getting in touch with the Soul can feel terrifying, as if our very core is going to disappear into a black abyss. The ego does not know or understand that more exists than its own story. It is important to remember that there is psychic energy in the formation and identity of the ego, and this can influence somatic, emotional, and psychological reactions—and we will explore many of these in

Part III of this book. As you work through the process, it's important to remember that the Soul is our spiritual vessel and our true identity. We begin to build our Soul relationship in order to know that we exist as more than our idealized identity of solely the ego. "The part of ourselves that we think we are is all that we are," says the ego. The Soul Voice knows better.

CHAPTER 4

LIFE VERSUS DEATH WISH

"To be nobody-but-yourself—in a world which is doing its best, night and day, to make you everybody else—means to fight the hardest battle which any human being can fight; and never stop fighting."
—E. E. CUMMINGS

"There are two basic motivating forces: fear and love. When we are afraid, we pull back from life. When we are in love, we open to all that life has to offer with passion, excitement, and acceptance."
—JOHN LENNON

"I think I can. I think I can."
—THE LITTLE ENGINE THAT COULD

The final thing you need to understand before you meet your Soul is an essential dynamic of human nature that influences each and every moment in your relationship to your Soul. Sigmund Freud, the father of psychoanalysis, postulated in his book *Beyond the Pleasure Principle* that all humans grapple with an unacknowledged suicidal death wish, which he described as the wish to return to "the inanimate." Freud, famous for his own death-luring cocaine habit, explained that this death wish surfaces as

25

a distractive tendency that pulls us away from the psychic strain born from the uniquely human problem of self-consciousness.

As in the cartoon battles between an angel on one shoulder and a devil on the other, Freud believed an inherent war exists between two fundamental drives: Eros and Death. Eros, the foundation of all life and the instinct for self-preservation, generates creativity, creates harmony, and produces the sexual instinct to reproduce. The death wish instigates habitual repetition, aggressive tendencies, and compulsive behaviors and finally implodes into self-destruction. The lure of the death wish appears as our often subtle but universal desire to seek out destructive states of unconsciousness. This death wish is what fuels the blocks we face along our path of getting to know our Souls.

Freud scholar and professor Christine Downing explains that the death wish consists of regression, avoidance, and resistance: "the voices in us that cry, 'leave me alone, let me have my way, don't make me change; let me stay a child, let me return to the womb.'"[4] Death wish is resistant to change—to the creative principle of life itself.

This energetic life-and-death battle is present in almost everyone, including me, all the time. We are all caught in the tug-of-war between the inherent pull toward "following our Bliss," as Joseph Campbell famously stated, and the hypnotic death wish that wants us to sheepishly follow the more predictable and accepted path.

When we reside in the energy of life wish, our internal narrative is confident, loving, and strong: "I am lovable. I can do this. I know the meaning. I feel the point." When we are in the clutches of death wish, our internal script becomes dismal and depressing. We start berating ourselves with negative self-mantras like "What's the point?" "I can't do it," "I'm not worthy of love," and "I am alone." The classic children's tale *The Little Engine That Could* portrays this archetypal struggle between life wish and death wish. As the story concludes, the little engine chooses life wish, triumphs over self-doubt, and makes it over the big mountain.

The death wish convinces us to judge our lives based solely on physical-world security and confirmation from others, while we identify as victims and nurse our wounds. It tries to keep us living solely in the realm of the ego, but our true Self knows that this is unhealthy. Caught in the death wish, we survive a never-ending *Groundhog Day* reality, trudging through our daily to-do lists with little joie de vivre. Life appears utterly meaningless and empty. We wake up dreading another sunrise, we clock in and out of work, and we trudge like zombies, lifeless, through the fluorescent aisles of the grocery store. We become vulnerable to addictions because we are exhausted by the weight of our days, searching for escape, desperate to fill the void. The cheeseburger, the new purse, or the porno becomes a holy moment of relief, a timeless break, in the tightening vise that life has become. All of life gets categorized as either suffering or pleasure. Ethan Hawke's avoidant and angry character, Troy, in the Gen X movie *Reality Bites* sums it up for us: "There's no point to any of this. It's all just a . . . a random lottery of meaningless tragedy and a series of near escapes. So I take pleasure in the details. You know . . . a Quarter-Pounder with cheese, those are good, the sky about ten minutes before it starts to rain, the moment where your laughter becomes a cackle . . . and I, I sit back and I smoke my Camel Straights and I ride my own melt."[5]

It takes incredible levels of discernment to clearly identify which drive is fueling us, because the death wish is so hypnotic and alluring. Downing refers to Freud's description of this battle as "twin brothers engaged in a dramatic struggle with each other and sometimes in so close an embrace that we cannot distinguish between them."[6] It is not so much *what particular action* we are doing as it is *what type of energy* is motivating us; in other words, *it's not what we're doing, but how we're doing it.* Are we motivated from a place of self-love or are we attempting to avoid our feelings by route of unconscious psychic anesthetic?

This essential question will surface many times as you begin to meet your Soul and move forward on your Soul Journey. As you work your way through the following chapters, remember that as a human being, you are wired to constantly feel this life wish–death wish battle. It is the battle itself that raises consciousness and helps to clarify the existence of the Soul to the ego.

This dynamic clashing between ego and Soul can create doubt or negativity on the path. In Part III, we'll go more fully into some of the blocks that can get in your way, and I'll teach you powerful yet simple techniques to overcome them. As you work your way through Part II, which teaches you the basic practices necessary to get in touch with your Soul, simply try to observe and then set aside the feelings of negativity, rooted in death wish, that may arise.

PART II

MEETING YOUR SOUL

CHAPTER 5

HAVE SOME HUMBLE PIE

"The Sailor cannot see the North—but knows the Needle can."
—EMILY DICKINSON

*"Recognize what is before your eyes,
and what is hidden will be revealed to you."*
—THE GOSPEL OF THOMAS

*"We have to be humble enough to understand
that there is something called mystery."*
—PAULO COELHO

Before we get in touch with the Soul, we often feel isolated and invisible. But regardless of these feelings, our thoughts, actions, and prayers do not go unnoticed. They are energetic beacons the Soul sees. She constantly witnesses our consciousness and takes notes. (Notes that, by the way, others can also get a hold of, if they so choose.)

When I do sessions with clients, it is through this energetic storage bank that I receive my information. The reason I can access your thoughts, and your medical, emotional, relational, and spiritual facts, is because you are sharing them with me, and with the world, all the time, through your energy field. The only difference between me and most people is that I have chosen to listen, on a deep level, to that energetic reality that surrounds us. But we can all do this.

To listen to the Soul, we must first humble the ego. The process of humbling is often embarrassing and painful. The truth does set us free, but first it often pisses us off. We give up the idea of who we think we are and focus on becoming who we actually are. Our words and interactions with others then become a reflection of who we are, not what we know. We give up the need to be "right" for the need to happily be ourselves. It is only then that being ourselves becomes disentangled from the need to be seen and understood by others. We realize we really want to know ourselves, truly and deeply, more than anything else.

Whether your ego understands it or not, our Souls are constantly engaged in energetic relationships. We are more like the character of the emperor in the story "The Emperor's New Clothes" than we are aware. We might think we are all covered up, wearing clothes, but, energetically, we are all buck naked.

The day I finally surrendered and had to humble my own ego and face the reality of the energetic world is one I'll never forget.

I was sitting in the classroom at my meditation school in San Francisco, where I was enrolled in the Clairvoyant Training Program. *Clairvoyant* means "clear-seeing," and the methods taught at my school utilize the imagination in order to "see" metaphorical, dreamlike imagery. We practiced with experienced "readers" and a teacher in order to begin learning when we were "off" or "on" with our psychic "hits," and to gain confidence and trust in our intuitive abilities. After the session, when we finished our readings, we were told to imagine walking down the hall and tapping the teacher on the shoulder to call her back into the room and let her know we were finished. I thought this was sheer insanity. I just didn't believe it would work. Who were these delusional people and why were they kidding themselves? They wanted to believe in magic.

Sitting in the lineup of psychics, after a classic "reading" for a new client, it was time to go energetically "call the teacher." I couldn't believe I was sitting there wasting my time with this shit.

In a fit of anger, I imagined myself going down the hall and up to my teacher, Julie. I saw her in my mind and said, "Julie! Get your *ass* in here!" I was pleased with myself.

A moment later, I heard running down the hall and the door was thrown open. Julie stormed directly up to me, pointed her finger in my face, looked me straight in the eye, and said, "Don't you *ever* call me like that again." She then abruptly turned and walked out of the room.

I was mortified. I suddenly realized I had been an energetic brat and needed to get humble, like, fast. I understood that we need to be responsible for our energy, even when we think we aren't actually hurting anyone.

We need to become energetically responsible.

Our energetics, which we constantly emit, reflect our true and underlying intentions. The Soul wants us to be spiritually conscious of our true intentions in order to enter into Her domain. When we become aware, open, and honest toward the energetic dynamics surrounding us, we humble the ego and become acquainted with our spiritual reality.

Humbling the ego is a process, and it is the first step in getting closer to your Soul. We begin by getting curious about the Soul: Who is She? What does She feel like? What is Her plan for me? What does my ego think and feel toward my Soul? Does my ego support my Soul or fight Her? How is my Soul trying to influence my life? Through this type of inquiry, we begin to turn toward Her. Our ego then bows to the reality of our Soul's desires and feelings.

Following are some of the exercises that I've found most useful for myself and for my clients in our attempts to humble the ego.

Humble Your Mind Motion and Prayer

I do this devotional practice frequently before prayer or meditation. Simply place your forehead on the ground as a physical reminder that you are relinquishing the addiction of the mind that prevails on this day. By doing this, you humble the mind to get it energetically and physically aligned with the heart, for just a moment. This quick process can have a huge impact on your spiritual practice. You can stay for five seconds or 15 minutes. Stay until you feel you have humbled the busy noise of the thinking analyzer in your head. After physically humbling your mind, set the intention on your Soul and pray: "Please remove everything in my life and mind that keeps me from You."

Humbling Inquiry

Spend some time thinking about what your Soul is. Answer the following questions in your journal: Who is She? What is Her plan for me? What does my ego think and feel toward my Soul? Does my ego support my Soul or fight Her? How is my Soul trying to influence my life?

Center

This simple meditation is a powerful way to humble yourself and get "out of the ego." This meditation shows us that as we consciously move our awareness to different parts of the body, we can experience different perspectives. With practice, you will be able to take a free vacation from the world, anytime you want.

Most of us spend the majority of our time identified with the ego mind (also known as the analyzer), physically located in the front of the head (between the temples). When we consciously move our energy, or awareness, back about two to three inches, to the center of our heads, we unkink the hose and allow the flow of energy to move freely down the rest of the spine (where the rest of the chakras, or main energy centers of the body, are located). Then we can relax back into the calm part of the mind, much like the eye of the storm.

Centering is great for getting neutral on emotionally charged topics. We still use the power of the mind, yet it gives us a wider perspective and allows us to view life from a different vantage point. Similar to peeling back layers of an onion, this meditation will allow you to continually discover your increased potential to sink deeper into this powerful place of knowing.

Throughout this book, I will often begin meditations with the instruction to "center." This is the centering meditation that I am referring to. A free guided audio version of this meditation is available at www.ElisaRomeo.com/MeetYourSoul.

1. Take several deep breaths in order to begin to slow down, relax, and feel your body.

2. Imagine a tennis-ball-size orb filled with golden glitter, located right in the center of your head. You can find this spot by putting your index fingers over the top of your ears and pointing inward. Their place of meeting in the center is where you want to imagine the ball to be. Physically, this spot is where the pituitary gland and hypothalamus are located.

3. Imagine your consciousness (your energy of where you are thinking from) moving inside the ball and notice how it feels to reside in this place. If you have been living from the front of the head, this move back can sometimes feel as if you are falling backward, and it may take a bit of time to adjust. For many it feels like sitting in a comfy reclining chair.

4. Inquire if there are any other distracting energies residing within the gold ball (like the presence of friends or family). If you do notice any other influences within the ball, ask them (with kindness) to leave.

Eye Gazing

We often hear people say that the eyes are the windows to the Soul. So it shouldn't come as a surprise that eye gazing, an ancient and powerful practice, can swiftly peel back layers of the ego. The intention behind this exercise is to have an intimate encounter with the "You" that lies behind programmed beliefs and egoic ideas of who you think you are.

To do this, sit in front of a mirror (preferably one that you don't need to hold). First, notice the exterior appearance of your eyes, the color and shape. Then allow yourself to relax and sense what you feel behind your eyes. The experience is similar to gazing at the Magic Eye posters where you relax your vision to allow the hidden image to appear. Like the posters, if you "search" for something, you will not find anything. Instead, you need to relax without expectation and allow whatever is there to appear. Also like the posters, you may find that you "get excited" when you begin to see something and you lose the image altogether. Keep breathing and try again.

It is normal to be pulled to focus with one eye at a time. Choose whatever eye you are drawn to. You are training your ego to surrender to the process. Your vision may become blurred or you may see the shape of your eyes as the rest of your face recedes from focus. Sometimes the light, or energetic body, reveals itself. In this case, the physical body appears to recede and what comes into focus is the bright, illuminated glow of your essential energy (also known as *chi*).

After some practice, you may even see other faces (from previous lifetimes) or images of your power animals in your own face. You can practice eye gazing for as long or as short as you'd like, but when starting out, aim for five to ten minutes. In general, the longer you go, the more the ego can relax into the exercise and allow the energetic information and feelings to surface.

An advanced variation of this exercise is to eye gaze with a partner, after you feel comfortable connecting with your own true Self. It is best to choose someone whom you feel incredibly safe and comfortable around, because of the intimacy of this exercise. You may notice some giggling as you both settle into the exercise. This is often part of the process.

Sit two to three feet apart in a comfortable position. Set the intention to see your partner beyond his or her ego. Relax your eyes and allow the images to present themselves. Roles between you fade away as you experience a true Soul-to-Soul encounter. After five to ten minutes, you can share what you saw with your partner.

This is a great exercise to begin to sense the energy behind the outer appearance. Over time you can practice with animals (be aware that for dogs, eye-to-eye contact can mean dominance). As you master the ability to relax your mind and feel the spirit of the being, you may notice you can also practice on eyeless life-forms like trees and flowers to feel their core essence.

CHAPTER 6

THE POWER OF PRAYER

*"Faith is taking the first step even
when you don't see the whole staircase."*
—MARTIN LUTHER KING, JR.

*"If the only prayer you ever say in your
whole life is 'thank you,' that would suffice."*
—MEISTER ECKHART

"We should seek not so much to pray but to become prayer."
—SAINT FRANCIS OF ASSISI

Many of us have so much stigma and heavy baggage on our relationship to prayer. Maybe as children, we were forced to utter memorized words without understanding their meaning. Maybe we were taught to beg for forgiveness of our sins from a fear-based God. Maybe we were trained to view prayer as a way to simply ask for things. But prayer is actually a powerful way to humble the ego even further.

Before I met my Soul, I only prayed on two occasions: after a horror movie (freaking out with insomnia) and during intense turbulence in an airplane. I was not brought up in a spiritually devotional household, and prayer was something I never seemed to need. In fact, I associated prayer with weakness: only the insecure needed to call on an imaginary friend for comfort. I was in control and too smart for those kinds of make-believe games.

Yet prayer is the way that we send smoke signals to the Divine. It is where we set and magnify our intentions about what we will manifest in the physical world. It is a resting place to feel our deepest hearts and a profound way to connect with our Souls.

The most potent types of prayer are not composed of ego list making, but allow the ego to surrender its role of micromanager of the universe. These prayers help us to "Let Go and Let God." In spiritual circles it is commonly said that "the most powerful prayer is a prayer of gratitude." When we reside in the energy of gratitude, we go back home to our energetic birthright of joy, peace, and inspiration.

Your Soul wants to be known. She wants to be in relationship with you. She knows how you want to be in relationship with Her. Relationships require communication and an investment in building the relationship. Prayer builds that relationship. Prayer is communication between you and your beloved, your Soul. She knows how She can directly help you live your fullest potential on the planet. She can restore your mind from the insanity of programmed illusionary thoughts to the emancipation of grace.

Even if you cannot hear Her right away, She is still there, always speaking to you and thrilled when you begin to speak to Her. Have patience—sometimes the relationship takes time to develop. Like a seed growing underground before proof of life appears on the surface of the dirt, there is often much more happening in our relationship to Soul than we at first realize. Her first communication may be through subconscious dreams at night or strong feelings and emotions we receive while praying. (All the exercises and meditations in this book are designed to help you to tune in and hear Her.)

Your Soul is your unique face of the God/Goddess presented to you in the highest individuated form that your ego can relate to. She is your spark from the great fire of "All That Is." You can trust your spark. She wants to heal your spiritual and physical dis-ease. It is through prayer that She helps you heal.

When you connect and pray to your Soul, you are also praying to God/Goddess/Source/The Alpha and The Omega. You are connecting to the spiritual reality that exists outside your ego. So when we pray to our Souls, surrender, and say, "Thy will be done," we are placing our trust in the Divine. God/Life Force/The Great Hum is in partnership with your unique spark. The will of the universe is your Soul's will.

One of the most powerful prayers I have seen consistently bring people relief is the Serenity Prayer. Although it was spoken before it was in print, this famous prayer was first published in 1951 by Reinhold Niebuhr:

> *God grant me the serenity to accept the things I cannot change;*
> *the courage to change the things I can;*
> *and the wisdom to know the difference.*

One of the reasons this prayer is so helpful and powerful is that it puts the ego in its place. It releases anxiety and allows the ego to take the backseat, by accepting change that is inherently unchangeable and empowering the ego where change is necessary. Feel free to alter the words and make it your own. Maybe there is another prayer that your Soul wants to send to you to give you daily guidance and comfort. The following exercises will help establish the bond with your Soul so you can call on Her for comfort and guidance.

Your Soul's Prayer

Write a personalized Soul Prayer. This can be your Soul's manifesto, the words that will call you back to your heart and Soul when you need reminding. Contemplate what elements are important for you to have in your Soul Prayer. The key element should be that you feel comforted and connected to Her when you say it.

Prayer Shawl

A friend recently taught me this amazing practice. She found a beautiful vintage tablecloth of Mexican fabric and turned it into a prayer shawl. She added fringe by sitting in devotion, tying colorful six-inch embroidery threads along the edges. Each time she threaded a piece of fringe she said a prayer. She was literally weaving the energy of her Soul into the beautiful fabric that would cover, support, and hold her for prayer. I love this idea. It strengthens the relationship between the physical and subtle worlds, marrying them together.

This is an easy craft project. You don't even need to have a sewing machine.

1. Find a beautiful piece of fabric you can drape over your shoulders—a piece that your Soul loves.

2. Purchase an embroidery needle and embroidery thread in beautiful colors.

3. Sit in contemplative silence and weave your prayers onto the edge of your prayer shawl.

4. Enjoy your shawl when meditating, praying, or sitting at your altar.

CHAPTER 7

SEEING THE INVISIBLES

"More and more the things we could experience
are lost to us, banished by our failure to imagine them."
—RAINER MARIA RILKE

"Imagination is more important than knowledge. For knowledge is
limited to all we now know and understand, while imagination embraces
the entire world, and all there ever will be to know and understand."
—ALBERT EINSTEIN

"Sometimes your only available transportation is a leap of faith."
—MARGARET SHEPARD

Your imagination is your greatest tool in your efforts to connect with your Soul. In George Bernard Shaw's amazing play *Saint
Joan,* the inquisitor taunts Joan and attacks her faith by saying,
"Your voices are only in your imagination." Her wise reply: "Of
course. How else does God speak to us?"

Imagination is the plane where we meet and engage with the
invisibles—*the very real but often unseen spirits, thought forms, col-*
lective energies, energetic information, and records that are always
available to us. The invisibles are a source of support and guidance
that often goes untapped. We are surrounded by helper spirits (our
spirit guides, angels, ancestors, and animals) and energetic information (the auric field, chakra systems, or the akashic records) that

can be extremely useful for our daily lives. The invisibles work just as hard in our lives as the visibles do, but the visibles are much more difficult to ignore; therefore, they usually get all our attention. Imagination is what allows us to plug into the energetic data bank that is always buzzing around us.

In *Women's Intuition,* Paula Reeves tells a story of a trip she took to the deep Australian Outback to visit the Pitjantjatjara tribe. The tribe members are known for their embodied intuitions where they receive messages telepathically; she refers to them as a "kind of Outback Internet." At the end of her visit she became seriously ill. All the men of the tribe were far away on a walkabout. Even though they were out of contact, the distant shaman knew instantly that one of the visiting European women was sick and needed healing. She writes, "He appeared at the flying doctor station shortly after I arrived in a Land Rover. Since he was on foot, that meant he would have had to anticipate my destination and leave before we had even decided to break camp."[7]

Others who have visited the aboriginals of the Outback have told stories consistent with Reeves's experience. Many accounts concur that the aboriginals believe that we, in our Western culture, have invented tools that do externally what they have learned to do internally. What we do physically, they do energetically. Where they are comfortable with remote or astral travel, we have invented airplanes. Where they use telepathic communication, we use telephones. It is not a matter of which of these methods is better or worse; it is a reminder that we can also access these energetic, interior realms.

In our rational Western culture, we exist in a climate of stunted imagination. We are not in conscious relationship with our inner worlds. Instead, we literalize and act out culturally dominant neuroses that present themselves symptomatically in pathologies like anorexia, sex addiction, or mood disorders such as anxiety and depression.

Mainstream society makes little time for and places little value on activities that nourish our inner landscape, things like active dream work, daydreaming, or journaling. Imagination is held with little respect. Children are asked with skepticism, "Did that happen, or was it *just* your imagination?" Adults who want to marginalize someone's position are likely to say insultingly, "He sure has a big imagination!" This immediately serves to categorize the person as naive and delusional.

Our Souls are invisible. But of course that does not mean that they are not real. The most challenging part of opening to an intimate relationship with the Divine is learning to trust the invisibles.

PERCEPTUAL BLINDNESS

Interestingly, one of the things you have to keep in mind as you're looking to get in touch with the invisibles is a phenomenon known as *inattentional blindness,* or *perceptual blindness.* I like to explain it like this: If you grew up in Los Angeles, you would be so accustomed to seeing the smog that you wouldn't notice it. Your eyes would have acclimated to seeing through the smog to pinpoint the forms of the people and buildings in your view. If you then decided to want to see the smog, it would be an adjustment to your senses. The same goes for learning to see the invisibles.

The world is full of stimuli. To avoid overload, our brains block some available information. We filter our environment down to the essentials of what we need to know in the moment. This is categorized by a psychological lack of attention that is not associated with any vision defects or deficits. The term *inattentional blindness,* coined by Arien Mack and Irvin Rock in their book *Inattentional Blindness,* covers the studies that investigate the question, "What is the relationship between attention and perception?"

Perhaps the most creative and widely referenced study on inattentional blindness is the "invisible gorilla test," conducted by Daniel Simons and Christopher Chabris.[8] Subjects were asked to watch a video of two groups of people passing a basketball around. One group was wearing black, and the other was wearing white. Subjects were then kept busy with the assignment of counting either the number of passes made by one of the teams or the number of bounce passes versus aerial passes. In select versions of the video, a woman walks directly through the scene, either carrying an umbrella or wearing a full gorilla suit. After watching the video, subjects were asked if they saw anything out of the ordinary. In most groups, 50 percent of the subjects *did not report seeing the gorilla or the woman with an umbrella.* The failure to notice these oddities while actively engaged in the focused task of counting the ball passes is astounding. The surprising findings indicate that perception is very much influenced by attention.

My father was the greatest critic and the greatest teacher on my spiritual path. He was a biochemist—a larger-than-life, rational man who was raised Catholic. He would tell stories about how he got all A's in Catholic school growing up, except for the F's he received in religion class—for arguing with the nuns. He didn't trust the "superstition" of religion and lived his life on the complete other side of the spectrum: as a skeptical, analytical agnostic. He only trusted what was provable.

One day, my father and I were sitting together in the living room after watching some TV. The topic of my energy school came up, and he said, "What is all this aura crap you talk about? Auras shmoras." My gut told me that my father was very intuitive; he was also, like many scientists, open in a way to the stark experience of phenomena. What he lacked was the confidence to interpret the data spiritually.

"Okay, Dad. We are going to sit here until you see an aura. An aura is just the energy field that surrounds a person, just like the bluish heat that surrounds a flame on a candle. You can 'tune in' to see the external layers of energy around a person."

I sat in front of a white background so that he would be more likely to be able to see it. We sat in silence for maybe five minutes. Tops.

"Okay, I see it," he said begrudgingly. "Yeah, it's kinda blue. I see it around your shoulder. It does look like the energy around a candle flame." I couldn't believe it! This was it. Finally my father validated me! He could understand the world I lived in, and we could interact in that reality. I was ecstatic!

"Well, I'm going to bed," he said.

"What? How are you going to go to bed after what you just saw?" When I started to see energy, I was ravenous for more information on the topic, for more experiences that explained what I was seeing.

"Well, it could be an optical illusion. Correlation, not causation." He got up swiftly and left the room.

Even though my father saw my aura, he disregarded the information because it did not make sense with his understanding of reality. We see what we intend to see, and, more important, we see what we put our attention on. Our literal view of the world expands or shrinks based on what we think we need to know. In other words, our beliefs, or interpretations, shape our perception of the world. If we do not hold the possibility of a particular reality, we close ourselves to an experience of it. We often see exactly what we are looking for.

Inattentional blindness leads us to disregard visual stimulus based on our beliefs and distractions. While these studies and stories focus on the visual stimulus in the physical and material world, the concept of inattentional blindness explains why we miss stimuli from the energetic and invisible worlds, as well. We miss the information and experience of our Souls, just like we miss the woman walking by in the gorilla suit. So busy are our days, we place little attention on the unknown invisible worlds around us that, with a little attention, could become very visible and known.

Through the small act of shifting our attention, we start to see what we couldn't see before. We begin to open up to these previously unseen invisible worlds by partnering with the imagination.

BRAIN STATES

The way to tune in to the frequency of the invisibles is to learn to alter our brain states. This is just what imagining does for us.

We often cannot access our imaginations because we are residing in beta state. Beta state is where most of us spend the majority of our days. This is the brain state of rational thought, analyzing, and managing our "to-do" list. Beta state is important because it helps us read a map, do our taxes, and keep track of our lives. We can make pros and cons lists from beta state, but beta state is not going to be where we receive our intuitive guidance.

Brain State	Cycles/ Second	Category of Consciousness
Beta	12–40	Fully Conscious / Awake State / Active Mind
Alpha	8–12	Meditation / Creative & Exploratory Visualization / Daydreaming / Light Sleep / Night Dreams / Connection to the Subconscious
Theta	4–7	Hypnosis / Deep Trancing / Deep Sleep / Lucid Dreaming
Delta	1–3	Very Deep Sleep or Unconsciousness

Alpha state is where we receive intuitive guidance and begin to connect to our Souls. We begin to move to alpha state by setting the intention to relax and raise our vibrations to receive higher levels of information. We consciously alter our states. Meditation, imagining, guided visualization, and creating art can all help put us into alpha state.

Theta state is the state that healers go into when healing. Children are more frequently in theta state than adults, which is apparent when you witness them completely enraptured by the creative story they are creating through imaginary play. In theta state we are available to have those incredible "aha" moments that can change our lives forever.

A famous and brilliant quote that is often credited to Einstein is: "You can never solve a problem on the level on which it was created." I am reminded of this concept frequently while meditating or doing energy work. When I cannot access my higher information, I remember I need to raise my vibration. What looks like a mess from outside the first floor may be barely visible from the penthouse. As we learn to meditate, we discover the elevator and get used to riding up to a wide-lens view of life.

When we learn to consciously alter our brain states, we can turn our often disregarded imaginations into tools to consciously interact, relate, and co-create with the Divine. We allow our egos to consciously partner with our Souls (and potentially other invisibles) to receive information from the subtle energetic worlds.

What is the difference between accessing these other energetic realms and just making up pretend stories? Imagination can be experienced in a passive or active state. When children play with their imaginary friends, they may not have a specific goal or outcome in mind. They may be having tea with a dinosaur. They typically let the playful scene unfold, acting out a conglomeration of things that happened to them that day or that they saw on TV. This would be imagining in a passive state.

The difference between imagining in a passive state versus an active, co-creative state is intention and practice. We learn to strengthen our focus, desire, and vibration to be able to receive messages from the Soul. Sometimes we need to spend five minutes viewing random images and "mental garbage" (which is really a conglomeration of ego influence and the invisibles) in order to clear out the channel so the more pure information of Soul can come through.

When I receive information from my Soul, it feels like something *Big—Is—Happening.* I yawn a bit more as my brain state shifts to another frequency. It feels as though the images I am receiving are a bit surprising and unexpected—not what I would necessarily think or hope for. Because of this, the quality often has a "foreign" or "other" element to it. There is also a feeling of neutrality; although I am in an active state, I am not using my energy to "make up" the images or information from my ego. There is a definite sense of receiving the information. I also begin to feel Her, my Soul's, presence and notice that my body responds with goose bumps or waves of a tingling sensation. Time slows down and the room becomes more poignant, sharp, and alive. Colors seem a bit brighter, and I feel as if I'm looking out at the same room from a different and more relaxed place in my eyes. My hearing seems to heighten; I may notice birds chirping or trucks passing on the street. As I allow myself to engage with Her, I experience deep and often unexpected releases, like crying or laughter, as I connect to emotions that are buried underneath the surface of my ego. This is not how everyone necessarily experiences getting information; it affects all of us in our own unique way. Pay attention to what happens specifically for you.

The list below shows some of the most common things that people experience when making contact with their Souls:

- The desire to frequently yawn (from adjusting our vibration to another brain state)

- Senses intensify (the room may appear brighter, birds out the window sound clearer, your tea tastes more intense)

- Body responses, including slowed breathing, goose bumps, or tingling

- The quality of time may slow down or you may enter into a state that feels timeless

- The images and information received are unexpected and may have a "foreign" quality

- A feeling of neutrality, as if you are receiving information, not creating it yourself

- A feeling or knowing that Something—Is— Happening (even if it is subtle)

- A feeling of Her presence

The first step to trusting your imagination is to get curious and playful toward it. Practice setting the intention to directly connect with your Soul. Through experience, you will be able to determine whether you are in the passive or active state.

THE IMAGINATION MUSCLE

The first time I sat in meditation and asked my Soul to reveal Herself to me, she appeared as an upside-down (inverted) triangle. I had been hoping to meet a legitimate and glorified Goddess, so seeing a triangle was quite a bummer. Since that point, I have come to realize, however, that this symbol is incredibly relevant and, actually, the most accurate clue that my Soul could have used to initially portray Herself. It took me years before I came across the meaning of the upside-down triangle in my reading—the inverted triangle is the symbol of the Divine feminine.

Because slow revelations are quite common, it is essential to approach your imaginative way of knowing with patience and trust; allow your relationship with your imagination to build. If you watch children play, you see quickly how imagination is our natural state. My son can turn the refrigerator in our kitchen into a tree as he searches for honey and just escapes a bee attack, or he can easily start a conversation with a variety of imaginary friends. My friend's daughter often comments on her mood by explaining how her "engine" is working. When her daughter notices her mother is anxious, she will say, "Your motor is really red and going really, really fast, and it's making banging sounds!" She uses her natural imaginative understanding of metaphor to make sense of and communicate her mother's moods.

It is only as we age that we forget to exercise the imaginative muscle; we begin to place emphasis on achieving over dreaming. Just like Puff the Magic Dragon when Jackie Paper no longer comes to visit and play with him, our imaginations are also forced to hibernate until we learn to play again.

To learn to play again, we must be willing to feel a bit silly, stretch out of our comfort zone, and check the inner critic at the door. We learn to switch gears, quiet the mind, and become comfortable patiently receiving information from our Souls.

When we practice visualizing, we build our imaginative self-esteem. We learn to navigate the subtle realms as they become more real and familiar. We start to feel sacred space enter into our days, and we notice the signs from our Souls—perhaps goose bumps when someone is talking, a heightened moment of déjà vu, or a synchronicity (a meaningful coincidence).

While strengthening the imagination muscle, there will be times that we'll be frustrated because we can't "see" clearly or we feel like we are making it up. Those times are unavoidable, and they're part of the process. If you find yourself stuck while talking to Her, you can always ask yourself, *Well, if I pretended to know the answer, what would it be?* This oftentimes loosens up the inner critic and allows a little more room for Her to communicate with you.

FAKE IT TILL YOU MAKE IT

In the beginning, as we build the imagination muscle, we need to "fake it till we make it." As we learn to trust our natural intuition and guidance system, we must go easy on ourselves. Learn to speak to yourself with kindness; remember that the goal is progress, not perfection. Imagine you are "leaning in" to these ideas and exercises. Do not concern yourself with whether or not you are *right*. For now, you do not need to *know* what is *absolutely true;* you only need to be open enough to start to play and experiment. You can always write off the whole thing later—after you explore it a bit. In the beginning, avoid perfectionism so there is enough opportunity for direct experience to occur. As you build the relationship with your Soul, you will begin to know when She is talking to you and when your ego is just pushing its own agenda.

Imagination is deceptively simple. You focus the laser beam of your attention on Her (or the idea of Her), and then you have done your part. After you set your intention, you can now just begin. Allow yourself to have an experience of Her. Learn to trust what you see, and know that She is sending it to you for a particular reason, even if that reason has not been revealed yet. You are now ready to meet Her with the meditations below.

Meet and Name Her Visualization

You can do this meditation by reading the following, or if you would like a free guided audio version (with some additional prompts), visit www.ElisaRomeo.com/MeetYourSoul.

1. Sit in a chair with your legs and arms uncrossed. Take several deep breaths. Put a hand on your belly and feel your stomach going out on the inhale and in on the exhale.

2. Remember that your Soul is the oldest and wisest part of yourself; She is always loving. She has wisdom and access to information your ego self can only glimpse.

3. Set the intention to bring Her forward. When you do this, you might see a color, feel an emotion, or see an image. This is how She is choosing to speak with you right now. Sit with Her and see if She feels familiar.

When you come out of meditation, take a moment to draw a picture of what you received. You can jot down phrases or words that come to you. You may not receive a clear picture, but instead get a color or a feeling. Draw or note whatever came through, even if it is just listing adjectives of how She felt. Try to capture, without judgment, whatever way She showed up for you. The more you can personify Her, the more you can identify Her energy throughout the day.

Name Her temporarily. The name can change, so don't be perfectionistic about it. It is just a way to call up Her energy for now. Sometimes the names are adjectives of how She felt (Joy, Grace, or Divine Fire) or how She appeared visually (Lilac, Pinky, or Rosebud). It is important to name Her to personify Her. This allows you to summon Her energy when you are separated or lost from Her in the daily stress of life. Characterizing Her helps you to remember and feel Her.

When you are finished, continue with the next exercise.

Golden Lasso Meditation

Yee-haw, cowgirl! Now that you have met your Soul, you're ready to know how to get access to Her anytime. Like a cowgirl lassoing up her cattle, this meditation energetically reels in your Soul, bringing Her closer to you. Because of your brain state's relationship to your consciousness, you need to raise your energy up to meet, hear, and know Her. Remember, you can't answer a problem from the same energy state in which the question was asked, so you need to travel to where She lives. She lives on a very different plane, so when you do this meditation you are actually *going to a different place*. You can think of it as free vibrational travel, and you don't even have to pack a bag.

1. Sit in a chair with your legs and arms uncrossed. Take several deep breaths. Put a hand on your belly and feel your stomach going out on the inhale and in on the exhale.

2. Imagine a large, heavy golden lasso sitting on the floor in front of you. Pick up the end and imagine yourself swinging it in a circle; get it really swinging.

3. Now look up (either physically or energetically) and see your Soul about three feet above you. You may see Her as a figure, a Goddess, or a colored energy ball. Swing your lasso up and around Her to establish the energetic connection between your ego mind and Her.

4. Now pull Her closer to you, right above your head. You have made the connection.

CHAPTER 8

MEDITATION

"Prayer is when you talk to God; meditation is when you listen."
—DIANA ROBINSON

"An error has occurred. Please check your connection and try again."
—STRAIGHT-UP WISDOM FROM MY COMPUTER

Many of my clients view meditation as a chore. It feels like another thing we "should" do . . . add it to the never-ending to-do list. But through the lens of the Soul, meditation is an opportunity to spend time with Her. It is a chance to have a date with your true Self. Meditation is a way to bring relief to our lives. It is the most luxurious, self-loving, and Soul-gasmic way to connect. It is the most revolutionary way we can love ourselves. In our busy, external, and hectic world, meditation is sacred time to fall in love with your Soul. We can't serve what we don't know, and meditation is an opportunity to get to know Her better.

Meditative states can happen naturally—during a walk in nature, while washing dishes and noticing the warm water and sparkling bubbles on your hands, or simply by taking ten deep breaths when you feel overwhelmed. Many athletes and dancers talk about the state of "flow" that comes through the joy of completely immersing themselves in the task at hand.[9] Some people notice that moving meditations, like Nia or tai chi, are a good way to begin. A regular sitting meditation practice can be extremely helpful for controlling anxiety, building mindfulness, learning to visualize, or consciously altering energy.

Meditation usually falls under two categories: engaged and observant. An example of an engaged meditation would be a guided or visual meditation, and an observant meditation would be a mindfulness practice such as witnessing thoughts without identifying the story they are telling you (for example, many Zen or Buddhist practices). Both types of meditation serve you in different ways. Observant meditations are great for building the experience of the inner observer, or Witness, while engaged meditations help to build intuition by receiving neutral information through pictures in the mind and consciously altering energy with intention. (For example, guided meditations have proven helpful and healing for cancer patients.)

I look forward to my meditation practice. It is a time when I allow myself to enter into a deep calming state and feel my Soul. I am frequently reminded that my Soul is always available, waiting for me to join Her even though the noise of my thoughts and emotions often block me from that direct experience. We need to be able to quiet the distracted, manic ego in order to be able to get the true information from our higher Self.

Sometimes when I am deep in meditation and either someone opens the door or the phone rings, I am shocked at the intense change between the meditative state and my normal waking state. It can feel like being hit by a truck when a thought comes barreling through the mind after I have been marinating in the calm sea of Presence. The feeling of interconnectedness with the universe that comes from these states is completely delicious.

Meditation can also be incredibly powerful. The Butterfly Effect, which is part of Chaos Theory, states that there is a sensitive dependence on initial conditions. In other words, a small change at one place in a nonlinear system can result in large differences in a later state. Named by Edward Lorenz, this theoretical example of a hurricane's formation was dependent on whether or not a distant butterfly had flapped its wings several weeks before. As with meditation, small shifts in consciousness usher in large changes on the physical plane as well as assisting in the total raising of consciousness of our species. When we are beginning to meditate, breaking patterns of unconsciousness and habit are challenging. Resistance is always greatest when we first venture out to make a change and take a leap of faith. We do not have the benefit of riding momentum in the beginning. We may have become numbed or accustomed to living with intense resistance toward our Souls and the present moment. Resistance is avoidance to flow. Momentum is merely the by-product of it. You get to decide if you want to benefit from the wave of momentum that results from conscious sitting. But don't expect to ride that wave immediately if you have just remembered the long-forgotten water.

It is the small battles that are the most critical with meditation. The heavens explode with applause when you conquer self-doubt in order to succeed in sitting for five minutes in Presence. This is a larger victory than the advanced mystic achieving transcendent visions of bliss. For the Soul, daily confronted with dormant and unpredictable powers of unconsciousness, small victories are huge celebrations.

The Butterfly Effect highlights the interconnectedness of the universe. A Bodhisattva who has taken the Bodhisattva Vow—in a quest to help save all sentient beings—is deeply aware of the reality of our oneness. Everything is connected and related in our energetic and nonlinear universe. It is not that the butterfly "caused" the hurricane, but its reality and small part in the larger play result in the hurricane. Without that flap the hurricane would cease to exist. And so, your small attempts at meditating can and will usher in hurricanes and tsunamis of powerful Love recognized by your Soul.

LEARNING TO GROUND

One of the most basic and powerful meditations that I practice is grounding. It is also a great meditation to start out with. When we can strongly ground, we create a strong platform for the rest of our inner Soul Work. What does it mean to be grounded? Well, when we are *ungrounded*, we lose our keys, stub our toes, and forget things. When my clients consistently practice grounding, I can see an incredible difference when I look at their energy fields.

Grounding cords are energetic tubes that look like pillars connecting us to the center of the Earth. Our grounding cords are our energetic connection with Mama earth. We have grounding cords that extend from our first chakra (or energy center) at the base of the spine and fall like a plumb line down to the center of the planet. You can imagine it as an extended tail. At the arch of each foot where our main feet chakras are located, we also cord to the center of the planet. These grounding cords run straight down and fall with gravity from the center of our feet. Grounding cords on our feet give us stability and permission to walk our paths and know our truths in the world.

Some people are naturally more comfortable with grounded energies and others deal better with astral energies. One person's Soul Path might be to "lighten up" and access the higher chakras, while another's Soul Path might be to ground and incarnate more fully into his or her physical body. Most of us are doing both to some degree but have a natural preference for one or the other.

I am geared toward the astral when it comes to meditation, even though I have earth energy pumping through me. The first time I energetically grounded during meditation, I felt heavy, dense, and a little bit suffocated. I needed to practice grounding, and at first it felt unnatural.

I've seen amazing results for anxiety disorders attributable to simple grounding cord meditations. I have one client in particular who cannot access her intuitive information when she is ungrounded, but when we energetically ground her, she is so clear, strong, and connected to what, just moments before, seemed unsolvable. We are often both shocked at how simple and powerful this exercise is and the intense effects it has on her perceptions.

Ground

You can do this meditation by reading the below, or you can get a free guided audio version at www.ElisaRomeo.com/MeetYourSoul.

Sit up tall in a chair with your feet on the ground and take ten deep breaths. Your belly should expand on the inhale and contract on the exhale. Be mindful to breathe into your belly; do not stop your breath short in your chest. Imagine the oxygen molecules floating all the way to the tips of your fingers and the tips of your toes. Do not skip the breathing. It is essential to shift your brain state.

Notice the feeling on the arches of your feet. This is the place of your very powerful feet chakras that run earth energy. You may notice tingling or see a color as you activate them with your intention.

Imagine roots growing down from your feet and moving past the layers of rocks and worms all the way to the molten lava core of the earth.

Feel the powerful earth energy from the center of the planet, and allow it to expand up through your grounding cords into your feet and up your legs. Allow it to move out any anxiety, stuck energy, or other people's energy that is held in your leg channels. Mentally check behind your knees for dark or gray stagnant energy.

When the energy has moved up to the base of your spine, your first chakra, send it back down to the earth, from where your tail would be if you had one. Like a pump, you are going to bring earth energy up your legs and down your tail, cleaning any anxious or avoidant energy out of your system. Do not bring the earth energy up past your first chakra into your belly. Keep it pumping through your legs.

Ground down in the present moment in the full power of now. If you are used to being more astral, this may feel heavy for a while until you get used to running earth energy. Stick with it and you will balance out your upper and lower chakras.

Breathing Meditations

The word *inspire* comes from the Latin *inspirare,* which literally translated means "to breathe." The English word *spirit* comes from Latin *spiritus,* "breath."

The most underrated and underused relaxation tool of all time is simply to breathe deeply. Everyone (mostly) knows this. Knowing is not the same as doing. But this simple technique can truly shift your energy. As my friend said to me the other day, "Inhale the good shit; exhale the bullshit!"

There are a number of different breathing techniques you can employ, so you just have to find the one that calms you the most and implement it daily. It can be nice to set an alarm on your phone or computer for several times a day for a gentle reminder to check in with your body and breathe. Here are some of the most common techniques:

- **Ten Simple, Deep Breaths:** Place one hand on your belly. Many people breathe in the chest instead of bringing the oxygen all the way down into the belly area. Breathe ten times, watching your hand rise on the inhale and fall back down on the exhale.

- **Four Square Breathing:** This popular breathing technique is named after the equal counts that it consists of. First inhale for four counts, then hold for four counts, exhale for four counts, and then hold for four counts. My favorite breathing exercise is actually a variation on this. I breathe out for twice the amount of my inhale: so breathe in for four, hold for four, then exhale for eight, and hold for four before I begin again.

- **Alternate-Nostril Breathing:** Alternate-nostril breathing instantly calms the mind. With your right hand, fold down your index and middle fingers, so your thumb, ring finger, and pinkie remain up. This should leave just enough room for your nose when you put your thumb to your right nostril and your ring finger to your left nostril. Close the right nostril using your thumb, and breathe in through the left nostril. On the pause between breaths, switch to holding the left nostril with your ring finger. Then exhale through your right nostril. Inhale on the same side, and at the pause, switch back to closing the right nostril with your thumb. Exhale through your left nostril. This is one round of alternate-nostril breathing.

Meditation: A Soul Meeting

Spend five minutes in quiet time with Her. Get comfortable and take several deep belly breaths. Try not to attach to any particular thoughts but feel yourself behind and between the thoughts in your mind. See this as sacred time to spend time with Her.

Get with the Program Inquiry

Because the Soul is invisible and elusive, it is easy to write Her off and not schedule Her into our lives. We have intentions of living a Soul-oriented life, but then our to-do list dominates and we prioritize the daily crises as more important. We need to schedule meditation and time with our Soul into our lives. Consistency is key.

This is simply a practical matter, so it's important to get to know yourself a bit better. What types of programs in your past have helped you to stay on track when you were trying to meet a goal? For example, have you ever made healthy food changes or created a regular exercise program? What type of motivation works for you and what type does not? Like with dieting, if we come from a fear-oriented place, we will have short-lived effects. How can you create a personalized program to meet with your Soul and give yourself support from a place of Love?

Personally, although it may sound silly, I really respond well to daily track sheets where I can see and give myself a gold star. This little visual motivation holds me accountable. Sometimes telling a friend what we are up to also holds us accountable. Rewarding yourself with a nice walk, a new scarf, or a massage is not only a loving reward but also great self-care.

You may be able to loosen up your routine once you have a more established relationship with Her, but in the beginning it is great to nurture the commitment with consistency.

What does your ideal Soul Program look like? How can you keep yourself accountable? What type of goals do you have for your relationship with Her? How can you practically and realistically get there?

CHAPTER 9

THE SOUL SPEAKS: SOUL JOURNALING

"The privilege of a lifetime is being who you are."
—JOSEPH CAMPBELL

"What we are looking for is what is looking."
—SAINT FRANCIS OF ASSISI

Who are you?

I am the whispering that allows you to know your Self. I am the ache to be free. I am the unforgettable and unwavering realization that you are already found. I am what you seek when you do not even know you are seeking. I am you at your most clear; you at your most comforted. I am what makes life worth living. I see the obstacles you face, and I know how to triumph against them. I am the yearning to open and relax.

To come into sanity you must release everything. See with fresh eyes. Bow down. Speak directly to the mystery. Stop interpreting. Know through the Knowing and feel through the body. Fling yourself into your most vulnerable places. Welcome the heart-yearning to be unprotected and fierce in the nakedness of your deep Presence. Stop comparing. Stop complaining. Be.

I stared at the page in shock. The voice speaking to me on the page was unrecognizable. It was decidedly not my own, yet also completely familiar. Rereading my journal, I didn't recognize the writing. As I wrote, the room had shifted in a subtle but powerful way; it had become imbued with a sacred and devotional atmosphere. Time had slowed as my perception of the still bedroom felt sharpened, clear, and alive.

I had been writing to this voice in my journal for several months. I began what I now refer to as Soul journaling in the vein of psychological inquiry, a writer's exercise of sorts. My background studying Jungian therapy had exposed me to the imaginary process of Active Imagination: exercises where we give our subconscious an opportunity to speak to us directly. While it started out as an interesting exercise, what I discovered was the most powerful tool I have ever found for talking directly to my Soul—getting to know Her better and being able to ask for Her advice.

I started by asking simple questions of interest to me, questions that felt urgent for the day: "Should I go to the movies this weekend with my friends?" "Why am I feeling irritated right now?" and "What was my dream about last night?" I would wait for a moment and "imagine" Her response. I was surprised that the information coming back from my inner character contained definite answers that were remarkably clear and wise.

I could not ignore the feeling that would come over me when I wrote to this voice. I could feel the difference between Her answers and my own. I felt compelled to ask this voice Her name. She told me it was Sophia. She explained to me that Sophia is the name of the Divine feminine, embodied wisdom, and the marriage of life force in physical matter. The wisdom from Sophia was smarter than anything I had ever come up with on my own.

Sophia, should I go to the workshop this weekend?
Yes, it is in alignment. But you do not need to go the second day.

Should I work on the second book or continue editing the first?
Keep cleaning up the first one.

I feel overwhelmed. How should I prioritize my day?
Prioritize me first, always. Always talk to me first.

What can I do today to feel better?
*Breathe. Enact simple, loving actions for your Self. Go
easy and know that this is a time of major transition. Write to
me. Look to me for answers.*

Why am I so burnt out?
*These are big changes that you are going through. You are
releasing lots of things that no longer serve you. You are leaving a paradigm behind. Everything you want is in this direction. You need to continue to plow forward. You feel beat up
by life. But it is not life . . . it is your deluded interpretation of
life.*

The predictions she made began to come true; the intuitions
about certain people's characters were proven accurate. And when
I followed her advice, I had a much smoother time than when I
ignored it.

Mostly, the comforting voice was becoming more and more of
a clear character, an always patient, loving, and trusted friend. As
the relationship strengthened, I began to feel the intimacy growing. I started to trust Sophia. I could no longer pretend this was
purely a writing exercise. I needed to understand just what and
who She was. I began directly questioning Her existence. It was
incredibly challenging to not constantly analyze and doubt Her.
I had to ease up on my inner critic and learn to believe that I
was actually accessing some type of true information. I was totally
baffled at the idea that She might be "real."

Who are you?
I am your Soul.

Am I delusional?
You are leaving illusion now. You are never alone.

How do I know I'm not just making this up? I don't feel like I Know it.
You have to actually stop and get closer to Know. You need to raise your vibration. You can't see clearly from down there; you have to be able to see through my eyes . . . and that takes a huge vibrational upward shift.

How do I trust when I don't?
Stop thinking. The place you know me from is the heart. The place you don't trust from is the mind. The heart always Knows. The mind is so loud it causes you to doubt the heart. This lack of trust in me is always a sign of mind dominance. You need to balance out the head–heart split. There needs to be equilibrium.

As the relationship grew, like any relationship, I became more comfortable going to Her, not only with questions but also when I was emotional and needed support. Her answers gave me more comfort and were more specifically tailored to my life than the feedback I received from friends or family was. When I was angry or frustrated, She would truly help me find my center once again.

I was no longer alone. I had discovered a spiritual adviser who was easily accessible and with me at all times. I noticed that I became calm, grounded, and empowered after speaking with Her. One of Her favorite things to tell me to do was to breathe. When I complained that She was always telling me to do this, She replied that I was always holding my breath.

There were several times that She told me things I didn't want to hear. She told me things about relationships that I would have rather denied. She told me to leave jobs that weren't serving me. Some of Her information seemed scary and challenged my ideas of who I was and what I thought I was capable of achieving. In these times I would rail at Her—"spiritual temper tantrums," we called them. She would never be reactive, but would allow me to vent. She would then calmly give me a practical step-by-step plan for how to dust myself off and move forward.

Sophia, I'm terrified to take this leap. I don't trust it. I don't know if I can trust you.

What are your other options? Either you can be connected to me and your heart-knowing or you can "go it alone" and live with stress. You know that your freedom lies in trusting. You have tried the other way, and where did that lead you? Feeling competitive, confused, and angry . . . Although it may be scary to leave the predictable path, everything that you truly want, everything you find beautiful, is in this new direction.

Do you think you are here to neurotically plan a life of stability and then feel oppressed by it? You are leaving a fear paradigm behind. Anywhere that fear has led you is now crumbling. What's happening is an expansion of possibility for your life. Your True Life. The other day when you were feeling your Self and had no fear, that is because when you live completely rejecting fear, it has no power. The power of evil rests upon the wavering of the decision to choose Love. Once Love is chosen there is nothing to fear. Really nothing to fear. Because nothing exists that is fear. It is not ultimately Real.

In time, the relationship became so strong I could hear Her even with the big and loaded questions of life. I began asking Her questions about the nature of reality, faith, and the universe.

What is the point of life?

We are all here for a reason. Life is not a cat-and-mouse game with comfort and avoidance. We are all dying. This is what everyone denies. There is no wisdom to the safe game. The safe game is crazy. We are all dying. We will lose all of this. Why would you make your choices around safety when nothing is safe?! Make your choices around beauty. Make your choices around authenticity. Make your choices about Love.

Shine your Love. We are here to do that dance. That is what you are here to do.

Are you ready to join me yet? At any time you can eject to your vastness. You need to have focus, discipline, and consistency. If you have no time for me, you have no time for you.

What I know now is when I am speaking to Her, I am not just speaking to myself; I am tapping into the ability to speak directly to my Soul Self. The paradox of Soul is that She is both closer and farther than we realize. We often chase our tails looking everywhere for answers, and yet when we finally turn to Her, She is so available and accessible it is hard to believe. This is not a writing exercise that connects me with a wise part of my subconscious brain; it is a way of channeling and connecting to the Divine impulse that is my spiritual home.

As I began to "descend" back into my ego after joining my Soul, I felt fear wash over me. I realized that because of the nature of the ego, I would have to work when I was back in my egoic state to remain connected to the feeling of Her. This birthed in me a serious commitment to find ways to connect with Her on a daily basis. I have found that Soul journaling allows my ego to serve its highest calling, to serve the captain of my ship, the CEO, my Soul.

My Soul is the most true direction to my life. She is the most powerful way I have to access my own "spiritual success" in this lifetime. It is only Her opinions that truly matter to me now. I realized there is no reason that I should not take advantage of the ability to do this and contact Her directly and as often as possible. If we want to be efficient spiritually, we will go directly to our Source. When we really wrap our heads around the potential for our lives and the direct connection we have to Divine grace . . . it is mind-blowing.

Knowing Sophia has emancipated me, I now live with the freedom of actually trusting Her wisdom, which is my highest wisdom. Her wisdom is uniquely authentic information specifically designed for me, sent to me in manageable bits geared for where I am on my path right now. This has allowed me the freedom to trust Her over the myriad external "experts" who, while well intentioned, do not specifically apply to my Soul Journey.

Experts can be useful for informational purposes, but I am guided by Sophia. Everything in my life has direction and purpose. The moments of confusion or uncertainty only exist when I fail to listen. She whispers in my chest, urging me along when something is right; She screams down in physical pain and blaring words in my head when I stray.

After I saw how much my life was benefiting from knowing Sophia directly, I wondered if I could teach this to my clients. In the beginning, clients called me for information and I would translate their Soul information to them. I started to try out different techniques to increase the relationship between my clients and their Souls. Soul journaling was the most effective tool that I found to ground and verify the validity of their Souls in their lives.

I was shocked at the beautiful and wise information my clients were receiving through this practice. One of my clients, Molly, did not think she was capable of getting information from her Soul directly. She was hesitant to sit down and begin talking to her Soul in her journal. I had to really push her to try it out, but once she did she was surprised by the results.

> Whoa, I just did your meditation and then immediately picked up my journal and got a direct download of information. That was pretty cool. I am not really sure exactly the meaning of what I wrote, but I am not going to overthink it. Suddenly I feel exhausted. That is some pretty powerful (and amazingly simple) stuff. I definitely need to start doing this on a regular basis.

The sudden exhaustion that Molly mentions is a telltale sign that there has been Soul contact. This is a common symptom as our ego minds try to integrate and process emotionally what just "came through" from Her. Especially in the beginning, as we build our abilities to jump from beta to theta brain states, we may become tired after Soul "downloads" and sometimes may need to crash with a nap. Here is the loving wisdom Molly received that day from her Soul when asking if she should move:

I am here, I am always here. Don't worry so much; your struggle will cease to be a struggle once you let go and give in to me. What does that look like? You will be governed by how something feels. It doesn't have to be some epic battle; it can actually be gloriously easy. Just give in and go. There is so much love out there for you, and you have so much love to give. Give up the traditional binds that are holding you back. You get to break free from the constraints. Go with your gut, and don't let superficial judgment prevent you from experiencing life. You are on the brink of a major change.

Don't fret about how or what it is going to look like. Just keep feeling your way, check in often, and go with the flow. The current will take you where you have been heading; time to stop resisting it. It's very exciting.

Sometimes the tone or language from our Soul Voice is different from the voice of the ego. Molly noticed this shift in vocabulary:

Apparently my Soul Voice uses words like "fret" and She is clearly not the next James Joyce, but it was supercool to have that all spill out without even thinking.

I have another client, Elodie, who received huge doses of validation, Love, and guidance when she began speaking to her Soul. Elodie expressed concerns about her relationship:

He's gone and it makes me feel sad, and I just am so sick and tired of feeling sad all the time.

But you don't feel sad all the time, and it's actually very vital that you feel this sadness. It's not merely a sadness that signifies that someone has left; it is a sadness that has to do

*with the original separation, the one that is much older than
your perceived feelings of abandonment around your parents.*

Why does it sometimes feel like he's just gone for
good?
*He's zoned out a little bit, and he experiences vacillations
in his own energy. It's not intentional, and on a Soul level,
he is omnipresent with you. He has not detached, but in his
day-to-day life, it has sometimes become necessary for him to
release his feeling states in order to simply function.*

That seems like he's just given up.
*He didn't give up, but he did (albeit unconsciously) give it
over to a higher power. He doesn't need to fixate on it all the
time because it's at the back of his mind. He did, as you said
before, "put it on ice."*

Elodie did exactly what I encourage my clients to do—ask the
Soul specific, practical questions regarding life issues. In this case,
Elodie asked about what steps to take next in her relationship:

Should I meet with him this week?
*You're overthinking it. A meeting will happen, or it won't.
But don't deplete yourself of your valuable energy. It's okay to
place limits on the amount of time that you have together, and
it won't affect the way that he feels about you, either. What
you need to understand is that you don't actually have the
kind of control over his reactions that you think you might.
His contacting you was completely independent of the kind of
effort you put in.*

I just have a lot of doubt over whether or not it would
work.
*Your doubt has to do with what has brewed in his ab-
sence. But spend time with him face-to-face and feel into his*

71

heart. Let your heart open, and you'll see what's true. Right now, you're lost in your own illusions and fears.

Because of the enormous amount of comfort that Elodie received from her Soul, she began to wonder if her Soul was simply telling her what she wanted to hear, not what was true.

I don't want to be given false hope.
Communicating with me isn't about being given hope; it's about being given the truth, which will always be given in the spirit of awakening you to who you truly are.

Elodie's passionate Soul, which she named Tango Dancer, became a constant for her. She had found her "inner guru," and I began to sense that she was becoming much more grounded, open, self-loving, centered, and empowered.

Elodie herself began to inquire about this new relationship with her Soul.

Is it possible for me to become overly dependent on you?
No, silly, because I am not separate from you. I am not a crutch!

Everything is changing.
Yes. Be grateful.

Another client of mine, Melissa, a writer, was shocked by how easily she could access her Soul in her journal. Melissa asked her Soul, Amma, questions about her writing process.

I feel awful about not starting my writing yesterday. I was frustrated with my computer problems and at myself for not being diligent. What do you have to say about this?
Your writing is already taking place. Trust that.

Am I lazy?

No, resistant. You are not lazy; don't call yourself lazy. You are fearful.

Should I still write my fiction?
Yes. You need to write the novel. You can finish it.

How am I doing so far? I feel anxious, why?
You haven't accepted that the writing is waiting for you fully formed. You are doing well. This is part of your writing process. It's all intertwined.

Be with me. Keep yourself open to receiving. Talk to me during the day. Take my lead. Getting work done is part of this experience, so don't become anxious about it.

I feel calmer now. Thank you, Amma. As you know, I have been feeling scattered.
Sit in meditation and breathe for a longer period of time than you have. You can listen to classical music if you want, but un-busy your mind. Then talk to me.

Melissa asked Amma about Her identity and the nature of their relationship:

Amma, are you my Soul or a spirit guide?
I am your Soul.

How do I know?
You can feel me.

Can I feel spirit guides?
Yes, but it feels different.

How do you feel with me?
Whole, complete, grounded yet light, in control, resourceful, loved—a deep real love, a love that has my back. I feel present, raw, spacious, protected—not that hurt won't happen, but more that I can handle it when it does.

What do you want me to know, Amma?
You are loved. Every fiber of your being is loved. Like a mother's love, my love is fierce. Always protected, always here, always available. Try to feel me today as you are walking around, doing your stuff. I am with you always. You may need to stop and feel into me.

Melissa asked about meaning in her life.

Amma, what am I meant to do?
Live a very full life. You have only been living half a life.

How do I live a full life?
Connect with me and lead from me.

Easy for you to say. I feel too old to be doing this.
Everything has unfolded for you in the right amount of time. You are in the right place. It's unfolding. Be here. Stay present.

Why am I so emotional, Amma?
Because you are hearing the truth and recognizing it. It's hard for you to cry because a stoic face is a face of protection. Chip it away; tears will flow freely . . . in time . . . no rush. You are doing well.

How do I know this is you and not my ego?
Because you feel me.

I do feel you.

Over the years, I have worked with many clients to uncover the voices of their Souls. I have consistently found that we all have access to this untapped wisdom. With a little intention and practice, incredible guidance, connection, and comfort result from Soul journaling. I have seen, over and over, clients who do not consider themselves to be writers, or even particularly spiritual, have astonishing results from journaling with their Souls.

Your Soul Voice knows that what you ultimately really want, more than anything, is to love your life now. You do not even have to know yourself or know Her or know the answers to your problems to be able to do this. You just need to allow room for the experience of life to show up for you now. You just need the cosmic slap upside the head to look around your room right now as it is: completely on purpose. You do not need to make anything happen. All you need to allow is the consciousness and Presence of who you really are, and the room for Her to shine through your eyes. Instead of looking with strained vision for answers, you allow Presence to present Herself to you, as She has always been, all over your room, all over your heart, everywhere. This is the life wish; the same deep truth that breaks through concrete sidewalks with small tendrils of roots pushing up from beneath the surface. Life finds ways to seep through the cracks. And because who you truly are is Presence and Love, the good news is you don't have to do anything about it. You don't need to make Presence or Love happen. You just need to stop pushing it away. You don't need to try to write to your Soul . . . let Her write to you.

WHY JOURNAL?

Sometimes people are confused about why we need to talk to Her. If She creates our very personality, why do we need to speak to Her and regard Her as something external on a page? Unless you are one of the very few individuals on the planet completely running their Souls—the energy of total and unconditional Love—through their bodies 24/7, Soul writing is an incredible healing practice to help "bridge the gap" between the ego and the Soul.

There are several important reasons why I encourage the practice of Soul journaling for my clients. The first is to practice clearly speaking to the most authentic part of ourselves. When we write from our Souls, we have access to specific answers to the grounded daily questions for which we all need answers. She is the practical workhorse that leads us back to our true nature on a daily basis.

We are filled with invisible but very real energetic complexes and programmed personas that can "take us over" and morph into ego identification. This can happen unnoticeably and in an instant. We may feel centered and whole in ourselves, and then we have a quick chat with our mother and suddenly an insatiable hunger comes over us as we reach for brownies. We may be in a great mood, flush with self-love and acceptance, and then one quick flash of the latest size-zero models at Fashion Week brings up self-hatred. To combat this daily energetic shrapnel, we establish a strong, clear, conscious connection to the Soul Voice. We do this through practice, a willingness to imagine, and a little faith. All the healing, love, and answers are closer than we can imagine, just waiting for us to come back home.

While we also can connect to our Souls through movement or art (which is also incredibly valuable), I still recommend journaling in addition. Although we can feel Her when we are dancing or painting, She gives us the nitty-gritty details on daily life through writing.

My observation is that my most disciplined Soul writing clients have the best success at deep, conscious, and established relationships with their Souls. For this reason, I encourage resistant clients to at least give it a try for a couple of weeks to assess for themselves if the writing has shifted their relationships with their Souls.

The second reason journaling in particular is so powerful is because when we "write it down," we create a concrete record of our Souls. Anytime we communicate or commune with our Souls, we shift brain states, making it much more difficult to recall details of what happened. This is the same challenge we face when attempting to remember dreams: though we have an incredibly vivid memory upon waking, by lunch we cannot recall the details to our friends. The dream is gone, except for vague feelings in the body.

Speaking to your Soul is similar to reaching your hand through a cloud and holding God. We are surrounded by fog, always—the fog of what we should be doing, the fog of others' opinions, the fog of the media. Our goal is not to clear the fog, but to remember there is a light, a warmth, the origin of our Source always available to us behind the illusion that it's not. Speaking with our Souls connects us to that internal Knowing.

When we record the Soul Voice in a journal, we bring Her into the light of day to keep Her there with us, integrated into the ego. We also get to enjoy the validation that comes when She predicts things. This helps build trust with the Soul as we learn that She is reliable and dependable.

Which brings us to the third important reason to journal: to build a deep and personal relationship with your Soul. Meeting our Souls begins with relating to the Soul. And like any relationship, it takes time and energy to build a strong and trusting connection. When you begin to journal, the relationship is unsturdy, like a seedling. Because of this, you shouldn't plant the young, developing tree of your authenticity in a windstorm. It should be planted in a protective area, shielded in a place where it has the time to grow its roots. Journaling is like building a little temporary fence to shield it from the hungry deer that would gnaw at its still-forming leaves. This is a private way to connect with your Soul and protect the relationship from scrutinizing friends or family members.

As we build the relationship, we withdraw our illusory projections from Her. We drop the *idea* of Her in exchange for the opportunity to *actually know* Her. The Soul shifts from being a concept to an experience, a constant, trusted guide and friend. A place we can receive Love when we are scared, alone, and humbled by life's blows.

Fourth, when we journal with our Soul, we learn to discern what is Her voice and what is ego. While dialoguing with the Soul is natural, it is also a skill we need to develop. It can take some time and practice to tell what is Her and what we are forcing and "making up" from ego. It is also more difficult to hear the Soul when we're anxious or in times of crisis. When we regularly practice, we learn to distinguish the mood, atmosphere, and body feelings that occur when we speak from ego, versus speaking from the Soul.

And, finally, because the information is on an incredibly high vibrational plane, writing helps to create the vehicle (like an elevator) by which we travel up and back down through our brain states. We become trained to open up the journal to comfortably and predictably arrive at our destination of Soul. The consistency of practicing allows us to get familiar with raising and lowering egoic awareness while "tapping in" to the realm of the Soul quickly and efficiently. With practice, your hearing will get better and better. Your Soul's answers become longer and more specific.

I can hear Sophia's answers for me so much more clearly and powerfully on the page than in my head. Even though I am clair-audient and can "hear" Her voice fairly loudly throughout the day, there is something particularly powerful about sitting with Her and hearing Her in my journal. Especially on big-topic questions, I often have no idea how She will respond until I actually pick up a pen and sit down to give Her the space to talk. Opening my computer or journal creates a Pavlovian response that allows me to feel Her strongly and distinctly. As soon as I finish my question, I can feel Her presence, excited and hopeful, waiting to respond. I remember one day, paperless and stressed out on a road trip, I frantically began searching around a restaurant for paper napkins because I needed to speak with Her at that moment, desperate to hear Her answers. This was when I knew I was hooked.

So once again, let's look at the reasons why we should journal:

1. To get practical answers to our life from the most authentic part of ourselves

2. To create a record

3. To establish a deep relationship with our Soul

4. To discern Soul from ego

5. To practice raising our brain state

An important note on privacy: Some clients hesitate to journal, fearful that their writing will be discovered by family members. There are two ways to solve this problem. You can get a journal with an old school padlock and key or you can create a password-protected document on your computer.

HOW TO JOURNAL

There are two different ways to speak with your Soul. The first is *dialoguing.*

Always start with easy questions. Ask what is present and pressing for you that day. Know that if you ask the "million-dollar questions," it might raise your anxiety, making it difficult to hear the answers. When asking questions that trigger the ego, we need to have a strongly established connection or we block ourselves from the answers. She has always been there, but you are just getting to know Her. Like a first date where we do not open the evening by speaking of our ex-boyfriends (hopefully), we want to start slowly. Do not open with "What is the meaning of life?" unless your relationship is already strong enough to ask Her that. If you can receive the answer, then you know *the bridge* is sturdy. You can find *the edge* of your relationship by where you stop receiving information. Start with questions like: "What are the things that I do that bring me closer to you?" (for example, yoga, dancing, meditation, walking with my dog in the park) and "What are the signs that I am connected to you? How do I act and feel?" (am more calm, feel joy in my heart, act patient).

As we covered in Chapter 7, it is essential to call Her by a name. If you haven't given Her a name yet, go to page 53 to do the Meet and Name Her Visualization now. If you'd like, you can ask Her directly what She wants to be called, but if you cannot "hear" her answer, feel free to just name her temporarily. The name can be vague (like Triangle, Love, or Grace). You can always change the name in the future, but name Her something now to build the relationship.

Another method to begin to hear the Soul Voice is the *Dear Beloved Technique.* Addressing the Voice as "Dear Beloved" (or some prefer "Dear One") sets a loving tone. Start with one of these personal openers and then listen and write whatever comes (without back-and-forth questions and answers). This gives the Soul space to speak freely, without interruption.

I recommend trying both methods, as they each have different benefits. Some people find it easier to use the Dear Beloved Technique, staying at the level of vibration of Soul and receiving downloads filled with heavy heaps of unwavering Love in a continuous stream of consciousness. The downside to this method is that we may be missing some of the practical, specific information that we receive when practicing the *Dialoguing Technique,* where the ego goes back and forth with the Soul. They each work different parts of our "energetic muscles." Ultimately, once they are both natural to you, ask your Soul if She prefers one way over the other to communicate with you.

Here is an example of the Dear Beloved Technique from my journal:

> *Dear Beloved,*
> *You are on track. You can't speed or slow the track. It is set up for you. You can glide much more than you have been. Give yourself over to the truth and faith, and trust in me. Allow yourself to be held. It is the greatest healing and blessing to be awake in the beauty of God.*
> *I know you are scared. There is a lot that still does not make sense for your "story." But start to find the reality in the feeling of my story. Surrender to it all. Surrender to the truth of what you know.*

If it feels weird or disjointed at first, remember to hang in there and "fake it till you make it." We need to move out of the critical analyzer and create room for the Soul to speak to us. Julia Cameron, in her amazing book *The Artist's Way,* introduces us to the practice of Morning Pages: as a practice in nonjudgment, write three pages every morning without stopping your pen. If you find yourself blocked at Soul journaling, this fast writing is a great tool to combat the inner critic. Even if you are writing to your Soul, "I don't hear you" over and over—stay with the process and keep writing. Sometimes it takes a bit for the ego to warm up to the response.

Oftentimes when I sit to journal, my ego needs a little time and space to vent before I get down to Soul business. Sometimes I need to "throw up" what is bothering me and get it out onto the page. I give myself five to ten minutes to vent about things going on in my life. I write down my to-do list and whatever else is bothering me. But remember, this form of journaling is not to stay in ego-land; this practice is to get closer to Soul. So I give myself ten minutes, tops, before checking in with Sophia for Her opinion on my troubles.

Before speaking with Her, I always center (page 34), ground (page 59), and do the Golden Lasso Meditation (page 54). This sets the "energetic stage" to hear and gives my unconscious mind the "thumbs-up" that we're about to enter into sacred space.

So now it's time to start talking with your own Soul. Check out the exercises below to help you along your way.

Speaking with Your Soul

In my sessions with clients, there is a running joke, "Can't you tell me what to do? You are just going to have me ask my Soul Voice, aren't you?"

More than half the battle is the consistent practice of the recognition and identification that yes, you have a Soul and She has an opinion on this matter. Turn to Her; let Her guide your life in this moment.

Remember, it takes time and energy to build the relationship with your Soul into a strong and trusting one. Even small amounts of time spent with Her are beneficial toward creating a more intimate relationship.

If it feels weird or disjointed at first, just fake it till you make it. It will become more natural as you practice. So grab your journal and try both the Dialoguing Technique and the Dear Beloved Technique that follow to see which works best for you. Here are some helpful tips to get you started and to help you along the way:

1. If you need to write about other things from ego, do it, but limit the amount of time you spend. The intention is to talk to your Soul.

2. Before you begin talking to your Soul—set the stage. Center (page 34), ground (page 59), and do the Golden Lasso Meditation (page 54).

3. Ask Her, or give Her, a name and address Her directly.

4. Write fast. Don't censor yourself or worry about grammar.

5. Some people like to write by hand; others prefer the computer for its speed. Do what's best for you.

6. Do this exercise during the time of day that most works for you. Some people feel more clearly connected to their Souls in the morning; some feel this connection at night.

7. Start where you are emotionally.

8. Remember that even if you don't hear Her clearly right away, She is hearing you, and you are building the relationship. Be patient with yourself, keep trying, and fake it till you make it.

Dialoguing Technique: Start by asking your Soul an easy question, such as one of the following:

- "What are the best ways for me to be with you?" (For example, walking in the woods, swimming, volunteering at a shelter, gardening.)

- "Are there any physical body signals that occur when I feel you directly?" (yawning, goosebumps, heightened visuals)

- "How do I act or feel emotionally when I am in your presence?" (I act more calm, feel joy in my heart)

After you ask your question, simply listen. If no answer comes, try an easier question. When you do hear your Soul Voice, make sure to write down what you hear.

Dear Beloved Technique: Set a loving tone to summon your Soul by opening your writing with "Dear Beloved" (or some prefer "Dear One"); then listen and record whatever comes. This gives the Soul space to speak freely, without interruption, and dose you with huge downloads of unwavering Love medicine.

A Soul-Eyed View

To get to know your Soul even better, ask Her about Her take on your life, as it is currently. She has the wide-angle/angel-lens view from the penthouse. She can see your current problems from the future, out of time, which can bring comfort to your wary ego. Take a current problem and have Her answer these questions:

1. What is this issue teaching me about myself?

2. What Soul Lesson(s) am I learning?

3. What do you know about this issue that I don't?

4. How can I be kind and loving to myself while in the midst of this lesson?

What Percentage Is Her?

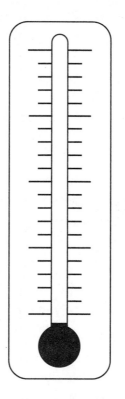

This is a great exercise to do after journaling to "get a read" on your Soul progress. After journaling, take a couple of breaths and ground yourself (page 59). In a meditative state, imagine an old-fashioned mercury thermometer and ask your Soul what percentage of the words coming through your journal are actually Her. "See" how far up the red fluid goes. This visualization allows you to track your progress and determine how pure your connection is, free from the influence of ego.

PART III

MOVING THROUGH THE BLOCKS

CHAPTER 10

SOUL ORCHESTRATION

"Meaning is invisible, but the invisible is not contradictory
of the visible: the visible itself has an invisible inner framework,
and the invisible is the secret counterpart of the visible."
—M. MERLEAU-PONTY

"Fate is like a strange, unpopular restaurant filled with odd little
waiters who bring you things you never asked for and don't always like."
—LEMONY SNICKET

Now that you've met your Soul through prayer, meditation, imagination, and journaling, it's time to investigate some of the common obstacles you'll face as you get to know your Soul better. The first concept, which often throws people a curve ball, is the topic of Soul orchestration.

The most important and life-changing realization I had upon leaving my body and meeting my Soul was the discovery that our Souls perfectly orchestrate the events of our lives. Later, I discovered this idea is not a new one. Plotinus (A.D. 205–270), one of the later Platonists, suggested that we choose the bodies, parents, places, and major circumstances that suit the learning of our Souls in a particular lifetime. Yet when we incarnate we forget that our Souls set up this particular environment, so that we can fully embrace the life experience.

When life is going smoothly, it is easy to accept the idea of Soul orchestration. If we get the job we want, find the relationship we had hoped for, or "randomly" run into an old friend in a foreign country, we trust that our Soul and the universe are on our side. In the rainbow leg warmers story in the opening chapter, my screenwriting client, Jennifer, discovered firsthand her Soul's powerful and positive manifesting as she was guided to meet the producer she had been seeking.

The Soul commonly orchestrates beautiful, positive, joyful experiences through which to usher us along our Soul paths. Yet our Souls do not always surround us with pleasant experiences, and this can seriously challenge our faith. Often clients voice their confusion—how can they trust that the Soul orchestrates the events of all of our lives when there is obviously so much pain and suffering on the planet? Why would the powerful Soul manifest and tolerate such painful conditions? Is the pain and evil in the world a result of a meaningless universe, a faulty law of attraction, or a dark force such as the devil?

The good and bad news is that being a human on Earth means you signed up to be, well, a spiritual badass. Spirits that have never incarnated as humans frequently admit to me that they would never contract to do a "Tour of Duty" down here. They tell me that even unconscious and lost humans are spiritual rock stars. Why? Because Earth is pretty gnarly. We exist as humans on this gorgeous spinning rock, which is a member of a light-based universe. This means that while we are surrounded by light, we are also surrounded by darkness (the absence of light). "Evil" *does* exist on Earth. Murder, rape, injustice, and war are still archetypal aspects in existence within our planetary, physical reality. The ultimate spiritual Truth is that only Love exists, but here on Earth, we are surrounded by shadows of evil. This cosmic setup is the perfect training ground in which to teach us the ultimate spiritual Truths. We are basically in spiritual boot camp, training to see in the dark.

To deny the pain of physical reality (the dark) is one of the main characteristics of a phenomenon called "spiritual bypassing," which occurs when our Spirit-to-Soul ratios are off balance.

The term was first used in the early 1980s by the contemplative psychologist John Welwood. In some of his spiritual-seeking clients, Welwood noticed a "tendency to use spiritual practice to try to rise above . . . emotional and personal issues—all those messy, unresolved matters that weigh us down." He witnessed in them a desire to "avoid or prematurely transcend basic human needs, feelings, and developmental tasks."[10]

Robert Masters's thorough book on the subject lists the symptoms:

> Exaggerated detachment, emotional numbing and repression, overemphasis on the positive, anger-phobia, blind or overly tolerant compassion, weak or too porous boundaries, lopsided development (cognitive intelligence often being far ahead of emotional and moral intelligence), debilitating judgment about one's negativity or shadow side, devaluation of the personal relative to the spiritual, and delusions of having arrived at a higher level of being.[11]

The Soul orchestrates painful and intense events in our lives in order to help us *consciously* integrate Spirit energy and avoid the flimsy and surface existence of a spiritual bypasser. Being human comes with this cold hard reality: we learn most quickly and efficiently from pain. Remember that famous line uttered by Westley, from the movie *The Princess Bride:* "Life is pain, Highness. Anyone who says differently is selling something." Wise words.

Why is this? Because 99 percent of the time, 99 percent of us would rather stay right where we are, sheltered and comfortable in our current ego thinking, than risk identifying with untested and uncomfortable new spiritual thoughts and behaviors. It's hard to teach an old dog new tricks—and the ego is the oldest dog around. Pain is an extremely efficient motivator.

But our cosmic "master" is not a sadist. The Soul's orchestration, though often painful, is motivated by an intense desire for our awakening. When we finally hear Her message, our suffering radically diminishes. We may still experience pain, but the meaning behind the circumstance is revealed. This leaves us with a deep feeling of connection and reverence for life. When we know Her we feel strong on our unique path, certain that even our weaknesses are essential and perfect for our tasks. We know we will be tested, and ego and Soul will work together to understand the meaning of the tests. We understand and are comforted that every moment is an opportunity to know and join with Her. The hard-earned result is the ability to see spiritually in the dark. Spiritual night vision is a major, heavy-hitting spiritual superpower, one that is admired in *any* universe.

Instead of seeing the coincidences in our lives as haphazard, mere luck of the draw, or cosmic flukes, we begin to filter our lives through the meaningful lens of Soul. Life literally goes from meaningless to meaningful. The term *synchronicity* literally means "meaningful coincidence." When we live the Soulfully awake life, the experience of daily synchronicities becomes a constant companion. We go from the astounded commentary of "No way! That was crazy! What are the odds?" to the calm and aware spiritual Knowing, "Of course!"

SYNCHRONICITY = MEANINGFUL COINCIDENCE

Frankly, most of us have a victim character lurking around the inner reaches of our mind, ready to pounce and confirm our fears at any moment. But what if we really, truly love and surrender to our current reality, complete with all its trials, tribulations, doubts, and worries? Right now. If you can do this, the voice of your Soul will rush in as the voices of doubt lose their power.

Your Soul is always trying to pull you home to your authentic Truth. She wants to release you from the pressure of family programming, from others' opinions and judgments. She is the most real and steadfast of all the energies flying around (and through) you on a daily basis, because She *is you* at root form. Everything else is programmed by society. What has been learned can be unlearned. We can kick the habit and reject our relationship to external influence. In every moment, She whispers to you: "You have a choice." You can look at yourself as a victim or you can learn the Soul Lesson that is intrinsic in this negative situation.

A beautiful example of this is a story from my client Ada. When Ada called me, she was suicidal. Although she thought of herself as a "pretty good-looking" woman, she had recently undergone nasal surgery to "tweak" her looks a bit and hopefully make her more comfortable in her body. The nose job went horribly wrong and she had the devastating experience of leaving the surgery disfigured and unrecognizable to family and friends. Her nose had collapsed and physically displaced her lips and other features. Ada explained to me that even though she had experienced abuse and poverty in life, this experience was by far the most excruciating. Seeing herself as a stranger in the mirror "floored" her.

Yet Ada's physical pain and desperation had also created an openness and readiness to receive some massive Soul Lessons. As Ada began to hear and feel her Soul, she learned that her Soul used her vanity as the means to get her to know herself as something beyond her looks. Ada wrote me a letter explaining the Soul Lessons she learned:

> Recently, I was having a conversation with my Soul (thanks to you, I do that now). I was asking why She decided to teach me the lesson through my looks. Ironic as this sounds (coming from someone who had a nose job), I always liked my looks, and I wasn't exceedingly vain. But She explained to me that my defense mechanisms around other things (my professional status, my intelligence) were too great; had She tried to teach me the lesson through those other things, I wouldn't have gotten it—I would've managed to avoid the gut-wrenching way the deepest lessons are learned. She had to go for something that I took for granted—that's how you learn about gratitude.

Ada planned a revision surgery that did not have a very successful prognosis because of the severity of the damage already done. We discussed staying close to her Soul for emotional and spiritual preparation before the surgery. Ada also found comfort from the spirit of her grandmother.

In the days toward planning my revision surgery, I was in close touch with both my deceased grandmother and my Soul Voice. Again, of course, this sounds superficial on the surface and, indeed, my grandmother and I would joke about the serious time she was putting in from the ether about my darned nose. My Soul Voice was there a bit, too, mostly as a sort of stern teacher. It was almost like She was giving me a passing grade on getting the work done from this lesson, but She was not particularly interested in me indulging myself about it. In fact, She was pulling me into another lesson. Namely, She very sternly instructed me not to "future trip." She meant, don't go fantasizing about how this thing is going to go. Take each step patiently; get through each day on its own merits. Don't try to force your will on the outcome. Don't tell yourself you deserve X, Y, or Z. Both my grandmother and my Soul kept giving me another message, too. They were saying, we are outside of time, but you are within it, so basically stay inside where you belong. LOL.

Okay, so surgery day. To give you some context, my surgeon had an extremely difficult job. He was attempting to re-create my old "look" while working with a nose that had been highly deconstructed from its original form. People are not clay. Molding flesh and cartilage is a scary and risky endeavor. The horror stories and failure rate of plastic surgery is so much higher than people know. I wish they were more informed because in a sizable minority of cases things go very wrong (e.g., 20–30 percent generally and there are even a lot of butcher doctors that repeatedly disfigure patients without penalty).

I tried to stay calm as they put me under. My grandmother was also in the room; she was behind me to my left side with a gorgeous rainbow presence. I woke up a mess, truly. Nervous and worried about how things had gone. I couldn't see my nose because it was bandaged. I wouldn't see it for six days.

Just yesterday, I went and had my cast and stitches removed. The doctor did it himself (which is unusual). It was painful. As he removed everything, the room took on an uber-calm feeling. Now, I will never look like I did—that's just not possible. But he achieved what is *very rare* for a reconstructive surgery—I looked like myself again, no more fear of running into friends and co-workers and them not recognizing me. He recaptured the essence of a face that no longer existed, and he simply did a beautiful job. Honestly, I may always look in the mirror and long for that old face that is gone, but at the same time, I feel like I can bear the difference with the understanding of how much it has taught me.

I now acknowledge my ability to connect with the spiritual world—an ability in myself that I was long skeptical about.

I know that I will have a fuller and richer life, and so, in turn, will the people that I love, because I have come to understand the importance of gratitude and am committing myself to gratitude as a way of life.

When we understand that the Soul orchestrates our lives and is very deliberate about the trials and the joys we face, we become the heroes and heroines of our life myths. We are empowered as we understand that the universe is conspiring to bring us to our biggest hearts and our highest goods. We are no longer caught helpless in the wheels of fate but thrust center stage into the role of our true Selves.

One of my ultimate spiritual role models, who showed me an incredible example of this, is my dear friend Emily. I watched her transform into a spiritual powerhouse because of one of the most painful human experiences possible: the loss of a child.

Emily was six months pregnant with her first child and everything had been going smoothly. She was ecstatic to meet the kicking baby girl growing in her womb. While attending a routine prenatal visit, the ultrasound technician became quiet. Recounting the story to me, she described it: "Deadly quiet. The worst quiet." She knew something was terribly wrong. She was taken to the doctor and told devastating news: her baby had a chromosomal defect known as Trisomy 18. Her heart chambers were not working properly, and the baby was not expected to survive the birth. Emily was suddenly put into the devastating unexpected situation where she would need to deliver her little girl within a week.

Emily went back home and was given a week to prepare for the delivery. That week was an intense spiritual time of contemplation and raw pain. Luckily, she already was equipped with the spiritual tools to understand that this event was happening for a reason. Instead of avoiding her pain, she knew to dive in with all her feelings to be able to receive the Soul Lessons.

> Waiting to deliver, I felt this responsibility. This spirit has chosen to come into our lives for a very specific reason. We thought: what are we going to do with that? I felt like a trailblazer navigating through a pitch-black, primal, authentic time. It was all sensory based. I gave in to being very instinctual to the process.

During that week of waiting, she found some comfort through visualizations and meditation.

> I would visualize my safe place. I went to my favorite big tree in Oregon. I wanted to see her there. I asked her: "Please show yourself to me, here." I received this incredible image of her as a huge spirit with this distinct third

eye. She was full of this warm orange fire. She wanted to hold me, which felt really good. I remember crawling into her lap. She was so soft and big and I don't remember any words . . . It was just really comforting.

As Emily described the vision to a family member, someone noted that the image that came to her had much in common with the Buddhist goddess Vajrayogini. This goddess purposely chooses wounded, damaged vessels to inhabit, in order to teach about living a full life through death. This image became incredibly meaningful to Emily's family's spiritual journey.

The baby did not survive the birth. Surrounded by loved ones, Emily and her husband named the baby Nora and bathed and dressed her. They hugged and held her frail little body before they took her to the mortuary. When they received the baby's ashes at home, they decided to hold the memorial soon after. Their authentic public grieving inspired others to heal their own old wounds.

I was so raw that it became an offering to the people who loved us. The memorial was for the people who didn't have an opportunity to grieve. We started a fire and there was drumming. An eagle began circling us overhead, while we stood on the beach. The participants wore orange, Nora's color. She felt like fire to me, her movements were so fiery and active.

People came to us and thanked us and wanted to grieve with us. The group healing was really special.

I asked Emily how she did not sink into a spiral of hopelessness during that time.

It just didn't feel like an abyss. We had a spiritual understanding that this was a "chosen" situation. I can see how for someone, you would want your life to end if there wasn't any feeling that there was a reason for it.

Now I still sing the Cherokee mourning song on her birthday. I used to sing it when hurting deeply; I would cry while singing in the shower. Now, seven years later, I sing it and it feels really different. It is a way to connect with her. I feel her lovingly when I sing it. It is no longer a painful attachment but rejoiceful.

Emily and her husband got tattoos of the goddess Vajrayogini on their backs in Nora's memory. Vajrayogini is also Nora's middle name. In their home, which is now shared by two lovely and amazing little boys, they keep an altar to Nora's spirit. I asked Emily what the biggest lessons were that Nora had taught her.

I learned how strong I am. I learned humbleness— how our story is one among many.

I learned that you can feel pain and not be pain. The story has lots of trauma and Nora doesn't want that to be the focus anymore. She doesn't want to be felt like that. She's taught me, "You can feel me and not feel pain."

I learned that I really love myself. I love myself so much that I can give unconditionally—to not think about myself, but about her. Just to celebrate with a sense of humor. It's really tragic and yet it's also *life*.

I learned I had the strength and willingness to be vulnerable to life's shifts—to not being set on one direction. In life, things can change so fast, it's really better to be malleable and hold on to the heart of it, which is: "I'm always going to be okay."

Emily has found purpose in helping families in similar situations navigate their way. She has helped educate and shift policies at hospitals for women receiving this type of devastating news, by creating bereavement packets for families to receive. She is also working on a children's book for the kids of families in these types of situations. (More information on Emily's powerful work can be found in the Resources section.)

When we are met with a challenging life situation, we need to ask ourselves, "For what purpose could my Soul have sent me this challenge? Although painful, what could She be trying to teach me that I could only learn through this particular circumstance?" We then begin to orient the ego to the underlying Soul orchestration.

DARK NIGHT OF THE SOUL

"What gives light must endure burning."
—VIKTOR FRANKL

Sometimes, on the Soul Path, our Souls orchestrate a test so great that it will make us question our faith, our sanity, and our Soul's plan. It will grind us to our core. These are not the small— or even large—daily problems of the ego but incredible tests of spiritual stamina. In fact, the point of the test is to grind us down. This period of testing is known as the dark night of the Soul. This term comes originally from a poem by the 16th-century Spanish poet and Roman Catholic mystic Saint John of the Cross, but it still applies today.

Through this test, the Soul sloughs off all nonessentials from our personality and life. It wants to get rid of anything that isn't in alignment with our highest good and our most authentic Self. A dark night of the Soul is a test that makes us shed the limitations of our personality. The test will feel like despair. During the dark night it is as if we find ourselves plodding along in a dimly lit tunnel underground. There is no validation or confirmation of the light in the scene that surrounds us. The test is not about where we want to be; it is where our Souls want us to be. The test is the process that transforms us.

It is important to remember that not all periods of depression, pain, or suffering are part of a dark night. The testing of a dark night is to ultimately wear down the personality so it can join with the Divine. So how do we know we are in an authentic dark night? Mystic Andrew Harvey explains that a true dark night will come with "remorseless ruthlessness while opening you up increasingly to divine consciousness. That's how you know you are going through an authentic dark night and not just another dark day in the life of the ego."[12]

Our dark nights save us from inflated, flimsy spiritual showmanship. These times of testing create the padding, the spiritual fat, that we must put on in order to ground and contain the incoming buoyant spiritual light. Although a dark night feels like a death or an ending, it is actually an initiation, a necessary process in order for the new life and identity to *begin*.

During a dark night, it is important to resist comparison to the uninitiated, whose lives may appear, especially at this time, to be overly blessed, simple, and straightforward. The uninitiated are easy to spot—they do not recognize the Sacred within the apparent mess and are unable to relate. They cannot acknowledge and navigate these heavy and solemn times. Beware counsel promising rainbows and unicorns from these spiritual Pollyannas at this crucial time. While they are well intentioned, if they do not personally understand the depth of the dark night, taking their advice when you are vulnerable can deter and even halt the spiritual birthing process. A common and current popular example is the use of the Law of Attraction to disregard the reality, significance, and spiritual development inherent within a dark night. Very much a real cosmic spiritual law, the Law of Attraction is but one cosmic player in a field of many. The Soulful orchestration and timing of a true dark night trumps the (often oversimplified) interpretation of the Law of Attraction to which Pollyannas so commonly refer.

When we honor our dark nights we begin to see how our hard lessons are kindling for the spiritual fire to burn off old ego habits that do not serve the Soul. It is in this way that She is a pyromaniac: starting the Divine spiritual fires that are necessary to clear and clean out the old, dead, rotting wood of our fears. We then have to not only notice the fire but look directly into it and feel its heat as we face our biggest demons. We come out on the other side as the badass hero firefighters that we are.

Soul Orchestration Inquiry

In your journal, write down three answers for each of the following questions:

1. What is a current challenge in my life? (Choose something with which you are presently struggling.)

2. (Now, take some deep breaths and set the intention to see the challenge through the perspective of your Soul, then ask this question.) How is this situation conspiring to free me? What are the possible Soul Lessons behind this challenge?

3. What arguments, feelings of injustice, resistances, or reactions does this challenge raise for me? How am I currently struggling against accepting these Lessons?

4. What would I feel like and how would my life change, if I could "get" this Lesson?

You can do this exercise now, but you can also use questions two through four whenever you face any challenging situation in your life.

Gratitude in the Night

If you've been through a dark night of the soul, you know that during these times gratitude feels next to impossible. That is why it is during this time we need to dig deep to find something to be thankful for. Sometimes the miracle is solely that we remember to be grateful in this moment, now. If you are in a dark night, list five things in your journal that you can be grateful for. This valuable exercise will help you see that even in the worst of times, we can find some goodness.

Darkest Before Dawn

Sometimes deep in the dark night, we feel that there is truly nothing to live for. During this intense spiritual test, it is good to remind yourself that (1) you are being tested and (2) this too shall pass. If you are feeling bleak, make your inner mantra: "There is a light at the end of the tunnel," "It's darkest before dawn," or just "Hold on." (If you are feeling suicidal, see the Resources section for further instructions on how to get help.)

CHAPTER 11

BURDEN OF PROOF

*"I do think science has the greatest need of loving skepticism, though.
As the dominant ideology of our age, it has a magisterial reputation
comparable to the infallibility accorded to the medieval Church. Its priestly
promoters sell it as the ultimate arbiter of truth, as an approach to
gathering and evaluating information that trumps all others."*
—ROB BREZSNY

*"For those who believe, no words are necessary.
For those who do not believe, no words are possible."*
—SAINT IGNATIUS

*"Science cannot solve the ultimate mystery of nature.
And that is because, in the last analysis, we ourselves
are a part of the mystery that we are trying to solve."*
—MAX PLANCK

Unfortunately, there is huge prejudice in the field of science toward "inexplicable" phenomena. Metaphysical topics that make up the field of parapsychology are often immediately cast aside as unscholarly and embarrassing. Energy anatomy, out-of-body experiences, and telepathic communication are often marginalized within the respected fields of research science. Anyone hanging around spiritual seekers will soon have incredible anecdotal evidence that validates these untapped human abilities, but don't expect to see this reflected in the mainstream media or the most popular scientific journals.

The scientific method is defined as: "Principles and procedures for the systematic pursuit of knowledge involving the recognition and formulation of a problem, the collection of data through observation and experiment, and the formulation and testing of hypotheses."[13] If the scientific method were utilized indiscriminately, it would heal much of the unnecessary gap between science and spirituality, and the "inexplicable" invisibles would eventually become explicable. Many would argue that there have been leaps and bounds in the past ten years to bridge the spiritual and the scientific worlds. Yet there still remains extreme cultural minimization in the coverage and handling of these topics by the scientific community. If we wait for "proof" from our rational culture to verify and legitimize the experience of our inner worlds, we drastically diminish our full spiritual potential. (For additional reading on this topic, please see the Resources section.)

The need for proof is one of the biggest blocks keeping us from directly connecting with the Soul and experiencing true spiritual intimacy. Spiritual intimacy occurs when we have a direct, personal, and loving relationship with the Divine. Sadly, our inner saboteur tries to stop us from experiencing this direct intimacy by needing first to control and understand. There is nothing wrong with processing information so that we can understand with the head, but we must also understand the limitations of a head-centric reality. If we need to understand at the expense of having a spiritual experience, we use our heads to avoid life instead of clearly witnessing and engaging with it. There is more than one form of intelligence and purely one way to know and explain phenomena. Often "proof" is used to justify what someone *believes* about the world. Yet spiritual intimacy is not about what you believe. It is about what you have *experienced* and know. It is about feeling the beauty of your potent Soul flavor on the planet and looking directly toward Her for orientation.

SKEPTICISM VERSUS CYNICISM

One way we can assess if we are using rationality as a spiritual defense is by understanding the difference between skepticism and cynicism. Skepticism and cynicism come from very different emotional states. I often tell my clients they do not need to throw out their skepticism. I want them to invite the ego to the spiritual party and integrate it into the process of spiritual development. Skepticism can help us to discern ungrounded charlatans and filter and integrate our newfound spiritual experiences into a healthy functioning ego. Someone can be skeptical yet still open to a spiritual experience. What is never helpful is cynicism. The energy behind cynicism is unvoiced and repressed anger attributable to trauma. We become cynical when we have been let down, abused, or betrayed spiritually. Many of us have not been seen or supported in our deepest and most authentic spiritual connections.

Of course, there is a continuum of cynicism: some individuals are only mildly cynical, while others carry much more extreme spiritual trauma. Yet, even when cynicism is mild, it is a call for attention and healing.

Mild cynicism is often due to a lack of authentic spiritual validation, reflection, and permission to explore from family or society. This form of cynicism is often displayed when individuals hear a spiritual story they find to be illogical or unbelievable. Instead of calm disagreement from a centered place, a reactive emotional charge erupts. It does not happen often, but sometimes when strangers find out I speak directly to spirits who have crossed to the other side for their living family members, I am confronted with angry cynicism. I have been accused of preying on the weak and susceptible. I have been attacked with sarcastic, demeaning jokes because what I say and do is "impossible." These righteous soldiers of logic do not know me, nor have they had any experience of my work, so their anger is not actually aimed at me personally, simply at the ideas I'm presenting.

At the other end of the continuum are individuals with horrendous spiritual trauma. Some were raised within a strict, tyrannical fundamentalist belief system. They were not allowed or encouraged to have their own opinions, feelings, or interpretations of their spiritual experiences. Others have been members of power-based "spiritual" groups (defined by extreme "groupthink") or even of actual cults who consciously used brainwashing techniques. I recently spoke with a client molested as a child by a "guru" who her parents trusted. She obviously had great reason to feel cynicism toward spirituality.

One predictable effect of trauma is that it can cause black-and-white reactions in the traumatized. It is important to *avoid disregarding all spirituality* because of spiritual trauma. Cynicism is proof of our intimacy issues with the Divine. Yet cynicism can become a gift if we see it as a message that something inside us needs healing. We can see it as a call to get curious and closer to our spiritual wounds. We need to give ourselves permission to heal the pain in order to open ourselves to direct experience with our spiritual source.

Cynicism often goes unchecked, masked as a valid, intellectual, savvy, and developed way of interpreting reality. We need to begin to ask, "How can I evolve spiritually and begin to heal my wounds? How can I avoid living in spiritual reaction and develop a proactive, healthy, and mature spiritual relationship?"

We do not have many models for mature, healthy, active relationships with the Divine. We have proof of fundamentalism, cynicism, and fanaticism; but what does an *ism*-free spiritual relationship look like? When it comes to spiritual intimacy, we have had a string of bad dates and spent lots of time alone—bitching to our friends and projecting on what *It* really is. How much have we allowed ourselves to just show up—open and curious—and allow ourselves to experience spiritual intimacy directly?

We cannot measure the immeasurable. It is only to be experienced. To experience a place, you need to go there, and you can't get there from here. Meaning, you need to alter your brain state, your psychic reality, your energetic vibration, to meet the energy and information of the place you wish to go. Otherwise you are just stuck talking, writing, and *believing* in things.

FROM CYNIC TO SPIRITUAL TEACHER

An astrologist once told me that my cosmic job within my family was to turn doubt into expectancy. Once again, my father, the eternal spiritual cynic, turned out to be a great teacher in my life.

My dad, a scientist himself, believed that when people die they fade to black as their bodies are thrown to the worms. He did not believe in reincarnation or an afterlife. After having a hard childhood, I think he was scared to have too much hope in the universe. He was a survivor and learned how to succeed through tough circumstances. He had created a beautiful home, a loving family, and a career in which he was allowed the freedom to work for himself and spend lots of time at home.

My father died, very unexpectedly, in 2006. One night, he and my mother were planning to watch a movie together. He went upstairs to use the bathroom, and he never came back. When my mother found him on the floor unconscious, she attempted CPR, but he was already gone.

I was living in San Francisco, and they were in the Seattle area. I remember waking up the day after Halloween, All Saints' Day, with 17 voice mails from my mother. I knew something was terribly wrong. I remember thinking, *I am about to go into shock.* Then, I heard my mother's voice on the other end of the line, "Come home. Dad died." And I slipped immediately into the cloudy fog of shock and grief.

I remember stumbling out of my apartment with my luggage after somehow booking an airline ticket. I drove to the airport and boarded my flight. I felt the most intense heaviness of emotional pain I had ever experienced.

Several months later, I was visiting my mom in Seattle, sleeping in the old bedroom where I had been raised. I was awoken suddenly out of a deep sleep at around 3 A.M. by a presence standing over my bed. I was terrified. I knew this entity had been watching me sleep. I didn't know how I knew that.

I went into my inner self, terrified, and asked: "Who is standing next to me? Is it a good or bad being?"

I got the news: *It is your father. He wants to see you.*

I opened my eyes and looked over next to my bed. I could see a figure outlined within the darkness of the room. I looked closer and could see atoms busily zigzagging around, making up the structure within the shape. I got the information somehow, the knowing, that he had worked very hard to send his energy into a form in which I could see him again. He had sent intention from his spirit state to slow his vibration down to a level I was able to identify with my human eyesight. My dad had come to me to comfort me.

But I sat there terrified. I told him, "Yes, you are my dad. But I am sorry; that is too much! I would be terrified if *anyone* woke me up standing over my bed watching me." I felt guilty that I had disappointed him and somehow fell back to sleep. (You know it's family when you still feel guilty about the relationship, even when they are on the other side!)

I was so confused by how much my physical self seemed to miss him while my consciousness and spirit knew he was still around. He would visit me in meditation and I could feel the bigness of his character, his strong, unique energy still present, while I would have nightmares where I was screaming out, "Where are you? Where have you gone?" I desperately wanted to hug him again and smell the warm skin on his neck. I didn't understand how my body needed to grieve his presence even when my Soul Self was still with him.

It was reassuring at this time to have several instances of "validation" of his spirit presence. My father had been the president and owner of a biochemical business that was left suddenly inoperable. None of my other family members is a scientist, and we had no idea how to continue the operation. I began to ask my father's spirit questions about the business.

One day, my dad told me, "Tell Mom to send the yellow envelope on my desk to the woman in Texas."

I saw a clear image of a big yellow envelope and the outline of the state of Texas. I told Mom. We checked his desk. There was a big manila envelope for a woman who lived in Texas.

In meditation, I talked to my dad. I asked him what his crossing experience was like. He told me it was extreme bliss to leave his heavy body and suddenly join with light energy. He was able to travel wherever he wanted through the power of his intention and experienced great joy in being able to watch over his family. He sent me an image of death: It was like a raindrop on the window of a car, where all the raindrops are falling down the glass, separate in their own identities and sizes. Then, at the bottom of the window, they join together into a puddle. He still had his own unique identity within the puddle but knew he was also the puddle itself.

I joked with him in meditation: "Who's laughing now at your daughter who went to wacky clairvoyant school? I'm the only one who can hear you!" I had to say I told you so. I think he was relieved to know he was wrong.

My father's death helped heal any cynicism remaining in me. Through our experiences of connecting on the other side, I discovered there were other ways of experiencing reality that were not only through the head. The following exercises will help you understand where you fall in this need for proof that stops some people from experiencing a direct connection to Soul. Once you know your beliefs, you can recognize when cynicism pops up and take it as a sign that something needs work rather than simply falling prey to it.

Proof Is in the Puddin' Inquiry

Take some time to journal about the burden of proof. Here are some questions to get you started:

- How crucial is external proof in your life in order for you to know something?

- How do you look for this proof?

- Does your heart-knowing "count" as proof for you?

- Can you think of a time you just knew something without having any rational proof?

Skepticism Versus Cynicism

Explore your own cynicism or skepticism through writing in your journal. What is your relationship like to your own spirituality? Do you feel spiritually intimate? Are there aspects of spiritual life (either your own or your friends' and family's) about which you find yourself feeling hesitant, reserved, or skeptical? What about cynicism? Do you find yourself having cynical thoughts about your own or others' spirituality? Cynicism is fueled by anger and can be a great helper to find the areas in ourselves that need some extra Love. If you can identify cynicism toward your own or others' spiritual path, see if you can find the anger behind the thought and weed it out. Were you spiritually let down, betrayed, or wounded in some way? Were you raised in a family with strong "spiritual programs" such as blind faith, an inability to allow critical thinking, or angry cynicism? Ask your Soul for Her opinion on your spiritual relationship, and if there is a specific way She wants you to evolve your spiritual development into the next stage.

CHAPTER 12

SOUL-NESIA

"Walk the mystical path with practical feet."
—ANGELES ARRIEN

*"The universe is not short on wake-up calls.
We're just quick to hit the snooze button."*
—BRENÉ BROWN

As we saw in the last chapter, because we survive in a mind-heavy, heart-weak culture, we often lack support for and validation of the incredibly subtle world of the Soul. A result of this lack of external confirmation is a form of doubt that I refer to as "Soul-nesia." This is an all too real experience for my clients and me. *Soul-nesia is when we intellectually disregard, minimize, and compartmentalize our intuitions and direct experiences of the Soul.* Instead of integrating these spiritual manifestations into a lived reality, they are written off as dreamed or imagined. We rationalize our understanding of events and diminish their significance.

In order to accept and integrate the Soul's reality, we must first learn to value Her reality. Like the character in *The Velveteen Rabbit,* we first ask the question, "What is Real?" In this classic children's story, the Skin Horse has a reputation for being wise. An old and well-loved stuffed animal, he has been in the nursery longer than any of the new, shiny, mechanical toys. After short-lived stints of ferocious play, the nursery children become bored with the new toys and break or discard them. The Velveteen Rabbit approaches the Skin Horse and asks, "What is Real?"

The Skin Horse tells the Rabbit that becoming Real happens when a child loves you. The Rabbit wonders if this is a painful process and if it hurts.

> "It doesn't happen all at once," said the Skin Horse. "You become. It takes a long time. That's why it doesn't happen often to people who break easily, or have sharp edges, or who have to be carefully kept. Generally, by the time you are Real, most of your hair has been loved off, and your eyes drop out and you get loose in the joints and very shabby. But these things don't matter at all, because *once you are Real you can't be ugly, except to people who don't understand.*"

As you build your relationship to your Soul, you become Real as well. You begin to emit a sense of inner strength as you realize that your identity is not dependent on external circumstances, but on the relationship with the part of yourself that is eternal. Like the love that sees through droopy eyes, we become initiated into a secret that only few truly Know.

Becoming Real is not for the fainthearted. There is a spiritual self-selection process; only those who are ready can fully experience it. This is why there is no point in trying to convert, cajole, or push someone toward consciousness. It is a form of violence to force someone to be ready. And you may find these same people don't accept or understand your new relationship to your Soul. But it is important to accept their experience with equanimity. Have the confidence that you know truly what it is to be Real.

The female Muslim saint and Sufi mystic Rabi'ah al-Basri lived in Basra, in the second half of the 8th century A.D. Rabi did not document her life through writing, but we are blessed with surviving stories of her devotion through the Sufi saint and poet Farid al-Din Attar. Rabi introduced the courageous idea that God should be loved for God's own sake, rather than out of fear. In *A Literary History of Persia*, Edward Granville Brown writes that Rabi was once asked, "Dost thou hate the Devil?" "No," she replied. They asked, "Why not?" She replied, "Because my love for God leaves me no time to hate him."[14]

This type of devotion is the ultimate way to combat Soul-nesia. When we love our Souls from a place of reverence, honor, and sacred respect, Soul-nesia doesn't stand a chance. It is crucial to make your Soul present in your life—visually, concretely, and practically. This creates an anchor to ground Her subtle reality into your physical one. These tangible reminders are imperative. And in order to weave them into your daily experience as much as possible, they must be fun, inspiring, personal, and characteristically your own.

I once heard a story of a sudden fire in a small town in Indonesia. The locals had time to grab just one thing out of their houses. Many of the people grabbed their altars. This story impacted me deeply. I wondered if I were forced to quickly take only one thing from my burning home, what would it be? The fact that the altar—the sacred space of spiritual devotion—was the one physical object these people grabbed showed the value and importance of those devotional objects. It displayed their connection to the reality of the invisible worlds and their connection to Soul.

Make Her Present in Your Life

One of the ways to ground the reality of your Soul in your life is to create a visual reminder of Her. Below are a few suggestions about how to do this. Do one (or all!) of these so you have a constant connection with your Soul in your life.

- **Soul Altar:** Make an altar to your Soul. Find a nook, a shelf, or a tabletop on which you can create a special altar that is in devotion of your relationship with Her. Decorate it with whatever feels most like Her: Christmas lights, photos, artwork, feathers, crystals, beautiful fabrics, necklaces, healing herbs, statues, things from nature (pinecones, rocks, shells), or Soulful quotes. You can put your most beloved books here. Whatever you do, make it uniquely your own. This is a great place to meditate and pray, to send additional loving thoughts and good vibes to your altar. Altars, like living things, need care and attention. Frequently check your altar for outdated items or move things around. Let Her know that you are honoring the relationship here.

- **Soul Collage:** Use poster board or a bulletin board to create a collage that represents your Soul. Grab a stack of magazines and catalogs. Ask yourself what adjectives your Soul feels like (fun, blue, joy) and allow Her to pick those images. Have Her guide your hands to the colors, words, or images in the pages that reflect Her. Rip out what you are drawn to without questioning or analyzing why. This can be the first thing on your altar to Her.

- **Soul Bible:** Although the term *bible* is most often associated with the Christian or Jewish sacred texts, it was originally intended to mean a "large and holy book." Create your own Soul Bible filled with inspiring poems, photos, quotes, and guidance from Her. Allow your inner guidance to find and tear out beautiful pictures from magazines that bring you to a state of reverence. Synchronicities are a wonderful thing to group together and list in one area of your bible. This helps create "proof" for your rational mind of the mysterious workings of the Divine, always available to revisit in times when you have forgotten. This tracking in your Soul Bible helps remind you that this world is miraculous, enlivening, and filled with miracles.

- **Soul Plant:** Plant a prayer. Find a seed or small plant and set the intention that you are going to nurture this plant like you are nurturing your relationship with your Soul. Send the plant Love when watering it. You can also put it on your altar or pray before your Soul Plant. This exercise creates compassion and connection between this plant being and the fragile and important growth that develops in our relationships with our Souls.

"Becoming Real" Inquiry

Like the Velveteen Rabbit, we all struggle in our own unique way with the question, "What does it mean to be Real?" Spend some time contemplating and journaling on the following questions:

1. What does it mean to you to be Real? How will you know when you have become Real? Do you know anyone who you think has become Real?

2. Who is your Skin Horse? Who are the wise people that you can go to with your questions about what it is to be Real? They can be dead or alive, mythic, or your flesh-and-blood neighbors.

3. If you were telling a loved child, friend, or family member about what it is to be Real, what would your wise words be? What would you say about the process of becoming Real? Is there anything you wish you could tell your past child-self about your own process of becoming Real?

Soul Supports

In psychology, we refer to things that support our healthy self-care as "Self Objects." What are some of your go-to Self Objects that connect you to your Soul? Think of the memories, places, songs, movies, and even material things that help you feel strong in your authenticity. In your journal, write what supports your relationship with Her.

Looking through my Soul journal, I see that years ago I wrote that the female-centric movie *Even Cowgirls Get the Blues,* the Goddess-oriented book *Dancing in the Flames* by Marion Woodman, and the incredibly colorful and emotional personal journal of Frida Kahlo all helped me to connect to elements of my Soul. Here are some questions to get you started:

1. What are the top moments when you feel connected to Her?

2. What are the movies or TV shows that help you feel Her?

3. What are the songs that allow you to feel Her?

4. What are the books that help you connect and remind you of Her?

Soul Models

What Soul Models help you remember Her? Who are those people, the real or imaginary relationships, who support your relationship with Her? These are not people to enviously compare yourself with, but inspiring people who act as energetic guides to help you get closer to your own Soul. Mine have been Mary Magdalene, Marion Woodman, Maya Angelou, and my fourth-grade teacher.

Write down at least four Soul Models in your journal, along with notes about why they hold this position in your life. (I would bet that the reasons they are Soul Models are also qualities of your Soul.) Once you have identified them, you can call on them in times of need. Imagine what advice your Soul Models would give you.

Soul Date

Allow yourself a half day or a full day of complete and devotional wandering with Her, allowing her to guide you. Before you leave home, state the mantra, "My intention is for this day to bring me closer to You, to strengthen our relationship. I invite You to lead." And then follow your intuition. What restaurant does She want to try? What does She want to do? Go to the library, browse a bookstore, sit at the beach, get fro-yo?

You can also have a shopping date! Go to your favorite store and listen to your Soul. What styles, colors, or textures is your Soul drawn to? You may be surprised to find that what She likes may be different from what your ego likes. Maybe she's a little wilder, more childish, or more playful than you believe yourself to be. Is there a specific stone in a crystal or jewelry shop that feels like Her? You can also, first thing in the morning, allow Her to choose what you wear. Stand at your closet and have her draw you toward what She wants to wear for the day.

CHAPTER 13

FOOL'S GOLD

"If the fool would persist in his folly he would become wise."
—WILLIAM BLAKE

"I welcome being called God's fool."
—SAINT FRANCIS OF ASSISI

*"Do not deceive yourselves. If any of you
think you are wise by the standards of this age,
you should become fools so that you may become wise."*
—I CORINTHIANS 3:18, NIV

It is no coincidence that the most common phrase of resistance toward the Soul that I hear in sessions is "I don't want to look like a fool." Or "I don't want to be stupid and foolish." This fear of the fool is the root of avoiding our Divinity and one major reason we're all so susceptible to Soul-nesia. When people discover what I do for a living, I often experience the amusing occurrence of strangers excitedly whispering their spiritual encounters to me in hushed tones appropriate for confessional. They are so visibly relieved to find someone with whom they can share their "foolish" stories. The other day at the bank, the teller leaned over to me and whispered in a conspiratorial way: "I have had some *incredible* spiritual experiences. But I would *never* tell anyone else about them! People would think I was crazy!"

In fact, recently, while headed over to see her doctor, I told my mom how common this secretive admission of spirituality is for me. "It can't happen *that* often!" she replied. Then, while we were speaking with the nurse before her appointment, it came out in conversation what I do for work. The nurse glanced down the hall to see if anyone could be listening and then whispered, "I have very weird intuitive things happen to me *all the time!*" After she left, my mom looked at me and said, "I guess you weren't exaggerating!"

Why do so many people feel the need to whisper guiltily about their own spiritual experiences? There is a very real stigma attached to the intuitive world of Soul, and no one wants to be perceived as "crazy." Yet when we allow ourselves to surrender to our path and the Fool's call, we consciously align with permission to know the Soul.

The first card of the tarot is the Fool. New life is always married to a large dose of archetypal Holy Fool energy. It is the cornerstone of courage—the bud of risk that is essential to leaving a preestablished mold. The Fool shows us how to engage with life in all its glory in order to enter into new worlds of discovery. The Fool saves us from lives of mediocrity. He is the strongest companion and encourager on the Soul Path. Without him, we would be lost, content to live the life others had planned for us. The hope is that we will be vindicated. The fear is that we will be wrong. In our fear, we often choose the death wish over the painful sting of being labeled as "wrong." We would rather be depressed than wrong. We choose the illusory reality of physical safety over being wrong. We are terrified at the image of becoming the court jester, making everyone laugh at the ball. We think that with the Fool, they are laughing at him, not with him.

The individual and collective energy that makes up the death wish is no laughing matter. When the death wish is present in a person, the matter of the body, the cellular structure, does not have the fluid energy of amusement coursing through it. The death wish sucks the life and light right out of the body, in exchange for the heavy energy of separation and victimhood. "I will never be caught fooling around." The death wish is dead serious.

THE SANTA WOUND

Interestingly, the pain of looking like a fool is experienced by many of us at a very young age. I can't tell you how many people I've talked to who remember exactly where they were standing the moment they found out Santa Claus wasn't real. Maybe the blow was softened with some talk about the "spirit of Christmas" being as real as the man with the white beard himself. But for many of us, that was the first time we realized we could be lied to and betrayed by our religious or spiritual authority, those colluders of fantasy themselves—our parents. We felt like fools. Maybe that moment was when we laid the first brick of our inner castle of cynicism. We might have become a bit rigid or defensive: "I'm not going to fall for *that* one!"

But if we can get beyond all of these mind trappings and start to surrender to what each moment has to teach us, we will always be guided. If you have ever been witness to a birth, you have felt the moment where the veil is paper-thin and time begins to melt. Right before the baby's first cry, there is a heavy, golden silence—time slows and the room becomes honey thick with awe, grace, and devotion for life.

If you have ever been witness to a death, you have felt the reality of consciousness leaving a body. You have seen the room become silent as you are left behind, while another being is going somewhere else. You can see the coldness in the body afterward, the lack of life. The question begins to fill your chest between tears: "Where are you? Where did you go?" You know that the personality was too full and too real to just disappear. Yet later, after experiencing death or birth, we become baffled by explanations. Words fail us. We often start to lose the feeling of the experience in the light of day. It takes a large dose of the Fool for our egos to accept the bigness of these holy experiences.

We have to open to uncharted waters that we do not necessarily know how to navigate. We need to take the foolish risk of holding space in our hearts that there may be more to life than our rational understanding can explain. If we deny this holy experience of spiritual validation, we feel alone, disconnected from our Souls.

I know from my own experience that it is possible to have a profound mystical experience and then have the ego resist, deny, or avoid the integration of the material into the personality. I was terrified to meet my inner fool; I held her back with a fearful rationalistic paradigm. Luckily, my inner fool was dead set on meeting me.

When I was 17 years old, my parents bought an intuitive reading and healing session for me as a Christmas present. Being rationalists, they normally would not have purchased an intuitive reading, but the session was up for bid at their Unitarian Church auction. It was donated by a fellow member named Stacy, so they felt good about buying the gift, as all the money would go to the church. I remember feeling confused when I opened the card for Christmas with the coupon for the reading. It seemed like a random gift that had nothing to do with my interests at the time. With my teenage know-it-all confidence, I dutifully showed up at Stacy's house for my session. She ushered me inside and took me to her studio, where she had water and tissues out. She pointed to them and said the tissues were available if I needed them—if I began to cry. I thought she was insane.

Within five minutes of sitting down, Stacy had me crying like a baby. She told me, in detail, very specific things about my life at the time that I had never told anyone. These were not generalities like, "You are a people person"; she relayed conversations I had had with my then boyfriend, revealing different elements of the relationship that I had not told anyone. She had popped my paradigm of reason with one little pin of energetic truth. I became paranoid. I could not hear what she was telling me because I was so overwhelmed by the reality that this was occurring at all. I stopped her.

"How are you getting this information?"

"From my spirit guides," she replied calmly.

"What the hell is a spirit guide?" I demanded.

She continued with the reading as my scientific and rational paradigm continued to unravel into bits all over the floor. This was before the days of the Internet, and I am sure I would have thought she had Googled me if that had been an option back then. It still would not have accounted for all the intimate information she seemed to know about me.

I left the session feeling naked and shaken. For many people, this discovery might not have been so intense, but coming from my rational and scientific background, I felt as if I were exiting Narnia or the world of *The Mists of Avalon.* She had audiotaped the session for me to take home. I immediately relegated the information from the session into a compartment in the back of my brain to a place labeled "Don't think about it." I slowly sunk into denial and repression. It took me a full year before I could listen to the tape.

What ended up bringing me back to Stacy was desperation. When I began college I had a wart on my left knee. I had shaved it and it had bled, spreading the virus and causing about 35 warts to pop up all over my left knee area. I felt like a leper. I had gone to doctors many times; they repeatedly burned off the warts with liquid nitrogen. I had so many warts and had done so many treatments that I now had third-degree burn scars on my leg, which I was told would remain for the rest of my life.

I remembered Stacy had said she was an energy healer, and since Western medicine seemed to be failing me, I thought I would try her approach. I would have tried anything short of a blowtorch at that point. I went to her office and lay down on her massage table. She began running energy into my left leg, with her hands placed slightly above my body. I felt relaxed as I slipped into a deep meditative state. I noticed flashing lights flickering in the darkness but did not pay them much attention.

"What do you see right now?" Stacy asked.

"Nothing. Just some flashing lights," I replied.

"What else do you see? I can tell you are beginning to trance."

The word *trance* scared me. I thought of out-of-control people becoming possessed or speaking in tongues. Nothing about trancing seemed in control.

"Nothing. Just some lights."

"Look harder!"

"Um . . . a chicken wearing tennis shoes." (This really happened. That is what I saw.)

"What else do you see?" she calmly pursued.

Suddenly, as if I were watching a Technicolor movie, a gorgeous tiger appeared right in front of my vision. My eyes were still closed. And I was now crying. I was terrified about what was happening to me. I had no reference point for seeing clear visions like this. I wondered if I had been drugged or if I was going crazy.

The tiger seemed to be trying to communicate with me. He was emitting a strong energy of loving compassion. He looked straight into me and then dived down through my body, dragging my consciousness with him. It felt as if we were rushing down a fast-moving tunnel, flying deeper and deeper into the unknown. I could see his powerful paws swimming, pulling us closer to something below us.

We landed in a setting that was dark and filled with other creatures. I remember suddenly having tons of information that I had no access to in my regular state. I "knew" that my warts were here to teach me a lesson: that I am lovable, warts and all. I began to speak of stories, small traumas, that I would not have consciously remembered. I knew I was releasing trauma that my body had been holding in my left leg, stories about mean comments an ex-boyfriend had made or daily annoyances that had energetically built up in that area of my physical body. I had no sense of time. I just knew I needed to get these stories out.

The next thing I remember is Stacy nudging me out of my trance.

"I have to go catch a ferry," she told me.

"Oh, yes, of course! How long have we been here?" I had no idea what had happened.

It had been five hours. Once again, I left Stacy's office feeling disoriented and vulnerable. But the next day the warts were gone. In a month, the scars I was told I would have for the rest of my life had disappeared. (Years later I discovered I had experienced a classic encounter with the shamanic "lower world.")

The experience revealed several things for me. The first revelation: an encounter with the Divine does not mean you have also done the work of psychologically integrating the information into your life and body. Even after this event, with proof of a medical healing, I continued to have profound spiritual experiences that I would write off, minimize, and disown. The ego was fighting for control of my paradigm. It didn't want me to look like a fool.

Do not let the fear of being a fool get in the way of your relationship to your Soul. It is through the experiences that bring this trepidation that we learn how to take risks, trust our instincts, and lighten up. The great news is that like the Fool, the Divine is not devoid of a sense of humor. As I often say, "The Divine is too serious a topic to take so seriously." So when you lighten up, you lighten up your vibration as well. The energy of amusement is a powerful healer. When you are laughing, the devil has no room to get in. When I am working with spirits that have crossed over and I encounter a dark spirit, I always rely on humor to get through it. Many dark energies thrive on fear, so if you are feeling scared, find a way to laugh. It is a spiritual practice to learn to find the Divine humor in this ridiculous comedy down here. Like I said before, we are spirits having a human experience—and the human part of the experience can suck. It can be thick with incredible evil, illness, and pain. Humor has a way of breaking through the matrix of our worldly stories—the stories that create our reality and our experience of it. When I have a heavy energy hanging out in my space, I go to YouTube and watch some funny videos, something along the maturity level of slipping on a banana peel. That, music, dancing, screaming—they are all amazing ways to shift energy.

One of my favorite spiritual superheroes is Saint Bernadette. Bernadette, from Lourdes, France, was known for her vivid visions of a "small young lady" with a white veil, blue sash, and yellow roses on each foot. This lady told Bernadette to return every day to the site of a grotto to be in prayer with her. Bernadette's parents were embarrassed by her stories of these visions, and the police even threatened to arrest her as she became more famous throughout her small town. The town was divided in its opinion of her. Some people believed she was crazy and should be put in an institution, while others began to follow her, believing she was truly witnessing a miracle. On a famous trip to the grotto, the little lady told her to "drink of the water of the spring, to wash in it, and to eat the herb that grew there." With these instructions, she began to kiss the ground. Soon Bernadette began to eat the grass and earth and rub the mud from the grotto floor on her face. The townspeople assumed she had gone mad and began to laugh and make fun of her. The next day, the townspeople were shocked when the muddy water had turned to a clear spring. These "healing waters" of the Grotto of Massabielle attract more than five million spiritual seekers a year, many of whom claim miraculous healings from the spring. Bernadette's story portrays the courage and heart of the Divine Fool—in the face of ridicule we can trust our inner knowing, and, through that trust, we can experience miracles.[15]

The Divine Fool is willing to take the leap of faith toward that one-in-a-million shot at true meaning in his life. He knows that rationality fails to find the cracks and crevices that create miracles. He knows that the safe game is not the game he wants to play. He would rather fail gloriously while chasing his own vision than live a life of smallness and conformity. He sees the humor in the plan of the universe—even, and especially, in times of crisis and despair. The Divine Fool laughs because he sees and understands the game. The game is to find Love when it seems the most unlikely or even impossible. He is a true Love Fool—following what he loves for the sake of Love. He marches to the beat of his own heart and knows that is the only sacred rhythm that makes sense. So don't be afraid. You can do this, too. And when you are willing to play this role, you open yourself to Divine connection.

Choose to Be a Fool

Do something that gets you outside your comfort zone. Wear a silly hat around town, speak in a wacky accent to your friends during lunch, or push yourself to bust a move when hanging with friends . . . Take a risk and see how it feels. Expect it to feel awkward and weird and do it anyway. You will find that you are still intact with all your dignity after the fact. The world will not implode if you feel like a fool. This practice allows you to be spiritually humbled so that your ego is soft and malleable instead of defensive, rigid, and protected. Know that you are building your tolerance for sacred, Divine foolishness each and every time you allow yourself to not take life so seriously.

The Energy of Amusement

This is a great visualization if you ever need to "lighten up" a room. Breathe and ground (page 59) and then imagine you are painting the walls of the room you are in with a huge paint roller. See yourself painting all the walls bright turquoise. Turquoise carries the vibrational frequency of lightness, laughter, openness, and fresh perspectives. Be warned: you or other people in the room may suddenly come down with a case of the uncontrollable giggles. (This is important to know if you are going to try this in a quiet setting.)

CHAPTER 14

FEAR GREMLINS

*"Most of us have two lives. The life we live, and the
unlived life within us. Between the two stands Resistance."*
—STEVEN PRESSFIELD

*"Your task is not to seek for love, but merely to seek and find
all the barriers within yourself that you have built against it."*
—RUMI

We all have Gremlins. Gremlins are the characters that live
within our heads whose sabotaging voices are present in our inner
dialogue. Gremlins aim for our weak spots, such as our desire to
not look like a fool. Gremlins are not afraid to hit below the belt.
Their mission is to block us from Soul. While the voices of our
Souls come from the energy of loving the mystery and beauty of
life, Gremlins are born from the death wish. The death wish does
not want us to be our true selves on planet Earth; it wants to destroy our chances of merging with our Souls.

In some cases, such as addiction, being under the control of
our Gremlins can result in physical death, but more often it results
in psychological and spiritual death. Gremlins command us to
live a life run by fear, instead of one fueled by the reasons why we
incarnated. Results can be depression; helplessness; or a safe, neu-
rotic, and unlived life. As you begin Gremlin work, you will start

to notice that many people live from an unconscious and unaware place rather than guided by the voice of the Soul.

EXPOSING YOUR GREMLIN

With my background in Jungian therapy, I am accustomed to working with the negative characters that live in our unconscious minds. I find that Active Imagination work—using the imagination to shed light on these inner lurking characters—is incredibly helpful. The book *Taming Your Gremlin: A Surprisingly Simple Method for Getting Out of Your Own Way* by Rick Carson outlines an incredibly practical and straightforward technique to personify our inner Gremlins.[16] Because these psychological complexes are tricky to identify, it is crucial to personify and name them when they speak to us throughout the day.

Gremlins are tricky. If we do not do the work of consciously exposing them, we often don't even notice them speaking in our heads. They masquerade as us, and we can't fight an enemy we don't see. The more descriptive we make our Gremlin characters, the more likely it is that we'll recognize them. This helps to raise the red flag the very first time the Gremlins whisper to us. We want to recognize and stop the Gremlins in their tracks the moment we hear, "You will never measure up," "Why even try?" or "You'll never succeed."

When I worked at rehabs, I would often use group therapy to help expose these tricky Gremlins to the light of day. Group settings are powerful because they provide an opportunity for us to see our lives through the lens of others. We are often most cruel to ourselves internally, and when our inner Gremlins are voiced publicly, the compassion and reflection from the group helps to break the cycle of abuse—sometimes this also transforms the group itself.

My client Shelby and I were standing in the center of a circle of 35 women. Shelby had been a crystal meth user for seven years. She'd come to our rehab program three weeks earlier and had started to detox enough that her moods were stabilizing. With the drugs moving out of her system, she had begun to see her life with sober clarity. She had lost temporary custody of her daughter, whom she loved more than anything. The girl was in foster care because of her mother's drug addiction. Shelby wanted to fight this addiction to get her little girl back.

Shelby was also anorexic. She severely limited her food intake and felt "grossly overweight." Shelby probably weighed 105 pounds; she used the meth to keep her weight down.

I knew that Shelby's life depended on facing her inner Gremlins. I looked her in the eyes. "Shelby, I want you to talk to me the way your Gremlin talks to you. Really give it to me. Yell at me the same way you hear that voice of hatred in your head."

"I can't talk to you like that," she said.

"It's okay. We all want to see how that voice treats you. We need to expose that voice in the light of day. Seeing the Gremlin for what it is takes some of the power out of it."

"Okay. You are stupid," she mumbled halfheartedly.

"Shelby. Your life depends on this. Your little girl's life depends on this. Talk to me like your Gremlin talks to you."

"Fine. You're a stupid piece of shit," she stammered, looking at me questionably, afraid she was about to be in trouble.

"Good," I told her. "Keep going . . . "

"You think you are so important, but no one gives a shit about you. You could die on the side of the road and no one would even blink."

"Yup. Keep going . . . "

"You are a fat, disgusting waste of space. You are never going to stay sober. I've got you under my thumb. You are going to dry out here for a couple months, and then come straight back to me and the meth. You think you are learning and growing, but really it's just a matter of time before you are a wreck again."

"What do you want from me?" I asked.

"Oh . . . nothing," said Shelby; she had fallen out of character and was talking to me like her counselor again.

"No, Shelby, I am you. Keep talking to me like that Gremlin. I am going to role-play you back. I'm speaking to the Gremlin: Gremlin, what do you want from me?"

Shelby snapped back into character. "I want you dead!"

"Will you finally be satisfied when I am?" This surprised Shelby's Gremlin a bit.

"Yes! I will be satisfied! You stupid bitch! I want you dead!" She said this, but it was not believable. Her Gremlin was cracking.

"I don't think you will be! I think I could die in the gutter and you would still be angry and vengeful! You can never get enough. Nothing will feed your hunger." I knew I was purposely angering her Gremlin. My gut told me to hold this newly emerging character with tons of strength. The room was silent. All the normally rambunctious women were watching with rapt attention.

"You stupid bitch! Don't tell me what I want! I will kill and destroy you! You are worthless! You are nothing!" I felt the force of her words through my body, and they were terrifying. I could feel the hatred shooting out of her, straight at me.

"What do you need from me?" I asked again, directly and with strength.

"Nothing! I don't need anything from you! *I hate you!* I don't need you!" Her Gremlin felt less like a demon now and more like a sad, angry little girl.

"I think you need to know that I am sorry. And that I love you." I was staring straight into her eyes. Tears began to well up and run down my cheeks. Part of me was surprised by what was happening. I could feel how intense this role-play had become.

"Don't talk to me like that, you stupid bitch! I don't need you! You are a piece of shit!" She was rambling now but losing steam. She was staring at me, surprised. Part of her was feeling the shift happening.

"I think no one heard you. No one saw you. You got angry because you were alone. You thought you needed to become hard to be safe. But your walls are holding everyone away." I realized I had to make it personal between the two of us for her to feel the Love. "I am sorry I didn't see you. I'm sorry I didn't hear you earlier when you were young. I love you. I love you." She was crying now, too. She was struggling to decide whether to look at me or to look away. Tears were streaming down her face.

I stared her straight in the eyes. "I love you." I could feel the power of this coming from my heart. I felt the energy of Love shooting through my body and dismantling the strong fortress of her Gremlin.

"I'm so sorry!" she finally said as she crumbled into tears. Her energy had shifted, and she was soft and undefended. She appeared humbled and exhausted. I looked around at all the women sitting in the circle of chairs around us. Everyone was crying. The Gremlin had been cracked open. Shelby now had a fighting chance to kick this addiction.

After this experience, I began to understand the potential strength of our inner Gremlins to control and torture us. The rest of the clients who were there that day would repeatedly stop me in the hallway between classes, saying, "I don't know what happened with Shelby, but she is totally different now." It was true. She was invested in her recovery, learning, taking in feedback, and hungry to heal. What was most surprising was how Shelby's Gremlin demonstration helped the other women become more curious about their own Gremlins and ultimately more compassionate and loving toward themselves.

Because of Shelby's brave role modeling, Gremlin work became very popular at the rehab. I find it to be extremely effective for looking at the inner cast of characters that try to sabotage us. And although one could argue that Shelby's Gremlin had more of a direct plan to kill her than most do, we all have inner hidden and unexposed characters that tell us we are not good enough.

The True Nature of Your Gremlins

Gremlins run on fear—this is how they are fed. They eat fear for breakfast, lunch, and dinner, and they like to snack, too. They assume you will not challenge them or make them miss a meal.

When I sense that a client has been taken over by Gremlins, it comes with an ominous feeling of possession. This is when I say, "The Gremlin is in the house!" This immediate feedback is so important in learning to identify the undercover and covert Gremlins.

Gremlins are resistance. The definition of resistance is "a force that tends to oppose or retard motion." Gremlins are the resistance to the courage and commitment to unfold into who the Soul wants us to become. Gremlins are very real and very tricky. They shape-shift and masquerade as internal helpers. They sound like the voice of reason. They tell us they are just trying to keep us safe, not make too many waves; they do not want us to make decisions we will regret later. When we finish a conversation with a Gremlin we feel depleted, anxious, competitive, and scared. They can appear sweet, as in the case of my client who named her Gremlin Smurf. The character appears helpful, like he is giving good advice, but then he slowly undermines and controls her—like her real-life mother does.

Humor is a great way to lighten up the heavy death wish from the Gremlin. I have a client who is battling addictive behaviors, and her Gremlin, Mary the Addict, looks just like Roseanne Roseannadanna, the popular character from vintage *Saturday Night Live* episodes. This helps her recognize her inner voice of defeat.

Sometimes our Gremlins are not strictly personal; they run in our families intergenerationally. The same Gremlin that haunts you could be the Gremlin that haunted your mother and grandmother. Recently I was working with a client who was trying to hear her Soul. Her witch Gremlin, Esther, laughed at her. "Who do you think you are? You don't *deserve* to know your Soul directly. You are not special. Everyone will laugh at you and think you are crazy." A toxic green slime covered her energy field, leaving her drained, weak, and unempowered. I received the information that this Gremlin energy of spiritual sabotage had been in her family for five generations. There was old religious and cultural programming that family members must go through a channel such as a priest or a church to know God—that it was scandalous to think she could feel God directly. She asked her Soul for Her opinion; her Soul calmly and strongly replied, "You are a child of God. Of course you can hear me directly." After she brought this inner war to consciousness, her ego began to accept this new, radical idea that she was deserving of direct contact with the Divine.

RECOGNIZING YOUR GREMLIN

Clients often ask me how they can recognize the difference between the Gremlin's voice and the voice of their Soul. The first test is to determine how you are feeling. The energy from the Gremlin will be constricting, fear based, controlling, and from a scarcity mind-set. The Gremlin loves to compare your life to the people around you and to talk in "woulda, coulda, shoudas." He will whisper phrases about the ex that got away: "What would it have been like if that had worked out?" or "If only you had moved to New York, gotten that job, had a baby . . . you would be so much happier now."

The Gremlin does not want you to own and acknowledge your life as it is now. He would rather tie you to ideals and ideas of life, instead of watching you live comfortably in the here and now. He would rather you be separated from yourself in visions of the future, regrets of the past, or hopes for your potential self than open and free to love what is around you now. The Gremlin leaves you feeling drained and exhausted.

The energy from the Soul makes you feel expansive, alive, bright, strong, and clear. There is often a feeling of settling into yourself. Even if She is telling you something that is hard to hear, there will be a quality of relief, of surrendering into reality with what life wants for you and is offering you in this present moment. The voice of the Soul is always loving and patient. She gives you energy. When we are with our Souls, we are infused with the Love from the universe, Love of our path. So just remember, Gremlins do the following:

- Lie. A lot.

- Leave us feeling drained, tired, dissociated, hopeless, lethargic.

- Question and doubt our dreams. (It's their job!)

- Compare us with others.

- Come from the energy of fear, aka the death wish.

- Masquerade as well-thought-out and smart ideas.

- Are best exposed through a character we can identify.

And the Soul does the following:

- Speaks our highest, most authentic Truth.

- Leaves us feeling empowered, hopeful, creative, authentic, and energized.

- Pushes us to dream bigger.

- Reminds us we are incomparable.

- Comes from the energy of Love, aka the life wish.

- Is always present but quiet until we turn toward Her.

- Is you, existing as an entity on another vibrational plane.

In every moment, either the death wish or the life wish is the rudder steering your ship through life's waves. Instead of being a helpless passenger, obsessed with the storm, you might want to check who is at the helm.

Face your Gremlins. Run toward your resistances. Look straight in the eye of the lie of your smallness. Know that any part of the story of you only exists in and of the mind. Seek the experience of yourself *now*. Shed what's covering your heart. Allow yourself pure realization of the Love that lives you.

Meet Your Gremlin

You can do this meditation by reading the following or, if you would like a free guided audio version, visit www.ElisaRomeo.com /MeetYourSoul.

Gremlin work is the most effective way to really personify and see the inner critics that we wrestle with daily. So grab some paper and some colored pens and get ready to meet your Gremlin.

- Sit in a comfortable, quiet place.

- Ground (page 59) and center (page 34) yourself.

- Set the intention to meet your Gremlin.

- Ask yourself what you currently beat yourself up about, if you compare yourself with others, or what you judge yourself on.

- Allow your mind to wander and see if you notice any feelings, visual pictures, or people coming into your imagination.

- Create a character that encapsulates the feeling of this inner critic. Is your Gremlin old? Young? Big? Thin? Hairy? Prickly? Smooth? Does it look like a witch? A monster? A snake? A sweet, cuddly teddy bear? What is its color? Size? Shape? Is it male or female?

- Take some time to draw a sketch of your Gremlin.

- Next, write the top five to ten phrases you hear your Gremlin saying to you.

You now have a way to identify this inner enemy of your Soul. Put your Gremlin sketch in a place where you will see it at home, perhaps on your altar. This way you will start to be aware of how much your Gremlin controls your daily decisions.

Gremlin Dress-Up Exercise

You can do this exercise alone, but doing it with a safe group of trusted friends can be entertaining and healing.

Dress up like your Gremlin. Put on the clothing and accessories that your Gremlin would wear. Act out and embody the Gremlin, saying the Gremlin's top five phrases that you hear in your head. If you are with a group, you can play the character of your Gremlin to each other. (Tip: This is a *great* character to play out on Halloween! You get to really know your Gremlin well when you play that role all night long in an environment where it is acceptable to play a scary role.)

After exposing the Gremlins through role-play, light a candle and send Love to yourself and each other. Set the intention for Love and healing to come to the Gremlins as well.

I suggest ending the evening with some chocolate and congratulating yourself for doing some hard shadow-work.

CHAPTER 15

THE ENEMY IS A GOOD TEACHER

"The enemy is a very good teacher."
—THE DALAI LAMA

*"I'll tell you who your soul mate is, tell me the one person who
has caused you the most pain in your life and that is your Soul Mate . . .
Because it's the person who has expanded your Soul the most."*
—CAROLINE MYSS

While your Gremlin is the negative voice inside your head, we
also have external voices testing us on a regular basis. We often
incarnate with the same motley crew of people in order to practice and learn orchestrated Soul Lessons. Our family, close friends,
and even enemies are the perfect "grist for the mill" to spark us
into knowing our Truth in a major way. These people know how
to drive us perfectly crazy while reminding us of our spiritual
Achilles' heel. Our enemies are perfectly chosen to help us know
ourselves.

Jesus was able to fully experience the Divinity of his mission
in relation to the contrast of Judas. We, too, have these characters in our lives. Their doubt in us activates our desperate, life-
dependent faith—in order to understand and experience what
we are. You never know how badly you want to live until you

are faced with your death. If someone is holding you under water in an attempt to drown you, the primal instinct to live surfaces as you witness your body fighting for breath. Sometimes it takes being betrayed to find our own inner loyalty. We learn about how we will not abandon ourselves because others have. We learn that we will now value our worth because our partner did not.

Often the peanut gallery that heckles us most surprises us at the end of the spiritual day by becoming our greatest cheerleaders. The hecklers often heckle because they sense the Truth in what we're doing. It's like the stern ballet teacher who is hardest on the most promising student. They often have their own large internal Gremlins that beat their own dreams down, so how could they possibly support ours? They would be disinterested or neutral if they did not have such a strong charge around our mission. The fact that they are so reactive points to the wound of their shadows. As Shakespeare once noted, "The lady doth protest too much, methinks."

They activate a very real fear in us that can leave us in energetic limbo. It is important to call upon the imagination to pull us out of this primordial sludge. If we ask ourselves, *Who would I be without this fear holding me back?* we begin to usher in the part of ourselves that is strong, connected, and waiting for us to join our Soul. When we are in the dangerous psychological territory littered with land mines of fear, we need to keep our focus on why we are fighting. It is tempting to lie down on the battlefield and surrender to the dominant energy of family and friends. "Why am I making all this fuss? If I could only be normal and follow the rules and be satisfied, I would not cause so much disruption."

But your Soul is betting on your Divine disruption. She's expecting you to leave a wake behind you. There's a pretty good chance that if there are no rough waves of doubt, it's probably not Soul Work. Some work of the Spirit might be able to bypass the messy task of birthing, but Soul Work is not scared to get dirty. The work of the Soul is the embodied marrying of our greater Self with our humanness. Our human experience is not lower on the hierarchical totem pole of spiritual judgment. We understand that we are here on purpose and take advantage of our reality now. We are not interested in escaping, spiritually bypassing, or ascending; rather, we are grounding our feet into the mud and saying to the universe, "You will see me now. I will see me now. I will be me now. Meet me here."

Soul Work activates our greatest fears and inner Gremlins' voices. We trudge into the shadows of the unconscious and face the collective trappings of judgment born from antiquated morality and social norms. If we decide the screenplay is not worth it, the business does not need to be built, or the painting does not need to be created, we are allowing our inner expression to be silenced. We have then become another casualty of fear.

GOING PAST THE JUDAS ON YOUR PATH

We are not our only source of sabotage; sometimes others may try to block our paths as well. When the fear is too great in our friends and family, they cannot join us on our Soul Journeys. We might need to go in and take stock. It is important to be fiercely protective of your Soul's Truth. Do you need to set boundaries with specific people at this time in order to make your dream come to life? Will you sacrifice listening to the voice of your Soul to maintain a relationship? Will their energetic cynicism activate your inner Gremlin to a degree that you are unable to finish the task? This stage of the journey is about accurately seeing others' motivations and being realistic about how much energy you have to manage it all. None of this needs to be personal. You are staying true to a more potent Truth than the agreed-upon one; you are staying true to the energetic reality. Your discernment here must be as sharp as the thinnest blade and as hard as a diamond.

Later, after the road is built and you have achieved success, you will find yourself surrounded by others in support. The skeptics from your past now earnestly believe they have paved the way for you, with no memory of their previous taunting. They only remember their roles as roles of encouragement—and this may very well be true on a Soul level. The frustrating thing is that their egos are completely unaware of their roles in your life. If you were to discuss with them how their doubt has paved the way for your faith, you would be met, most likely, with blank stares. You must know that you can never get their validation to the degree you feel you need it. This fight is only between you and you. They may have been the personifications of your inner critic—holding the place marker of your doubt and your belief of what was impossible. If you override this fear by honoring that nagging persistent reality of what you know in your deepest Self, you will succeed spiritually. You will give your Self an opportunity to know and meet itself here.

These Judas characters are Soul orchestrated by us and for us to continue to point us in the right direction—the direction home, toward our potential. The fear that they carry encourages the Love we sense to birth itself on the planet for all to see. We might have very real human scars that need to heal, but the spiritual Self is always whole, intact, and emanating Love. It is an annoyingly ironic spiritual Truth that when we allow ourselves to blaze our Souls' paths we are often met by the confusion of friends and family. We cannot expect them to ever truly understand our mission, because it is not their path. They often play the part of the thorn in your side, but on a Soul level, they're hoping you prove them wrong.

Who's Your Judas?

Spend some time with your journal contemplating the following questions: Who has triggered you the most to know your Truth? Are there friends or family who drive you up a wall and force you into your Knowing? From a Soul-eyed view, what is the "contract" for these relationships? What do you need to know wholly and completely to unravel the karma between you?

Become the Heroine of Your Story

Think of a challenging story from your life—this can be an incident from childhood or a present-day issue—and follow this process:

1. First, write just the facts of the story or what happened. You can go into as much or as little detail as you would like. (For example, I was never invited to my neighbor's birthday party.)

2. Next, write the story as a victim. (For example, I never got to play in their pool and was always ignored by the other neighborhood kids. It hurt my self-esteem and made me always fearful of creating new friendships.) Don't stop here!

3. Finally, write the story as the hero/heroine. (For example, not being invited by the neighbo=-rhood kids to play encouraged my love of art and gave me many hours to work on my painting skills. I gained independence and learned to value my time with myself.)

You can find a free in-depth and expanded version of this writing exercise at www.ElisaRomeo.com/freebies.

CHAPTER 16

DIVINE SHIT STORMS

"Breakdowns can create breakthroughs.
Things fall apart so things can fall together."
—ANONYMOUS

"Row, row, row your boat gently down the stream.
Merrily, merrily, merrily, merrily, life is but a dream."
—POPULAR NURSERY RHYME

As the Soul works to integrate and make conscious all aspects of our lives, we meet another challenge: facing the unconscious material we would rather avoid, repress, and disown. In other words, in order to meet our Souls we need to claim our shit. It becomes a bit easier to face the shit storms of our lives when we recognize the meaning and direction inherently within them.

Although it is potentially distasteful, I use the word *shit* very purposely and consciously. Frequently when my clients are overwhelmed by life, they say, "My life is shit." Or, "What happened was total bullshit." In dreams, when shit appears, it often represents the shadow parts of ourselves—the disowned part of our personality or our life that is not socially or personally acceptable.

Many therapists who work with the shadow self know that it is often helpful to investigate the unconscious areas in our waking lives in the same way we would with a dream. We can begin to amplify and interpret signs and symbols, just as we would a dream image, in order to understand the Soul meaning inherent within them. Here is living proof of Jung's theory that "what does not come to us through consciousness shows up through fate."[17]

My four-year-old son is obsessed with poop, at the moment. It started as a parental attempt to not make part of his body's natural expulsion system "bad" or "wrong"—so you could say we tried to be "poop positive." We showed him children's books on going to the potty and approached the subject with exaggerated tolerance.

During this poop-centric developmental phase, one day we ended up talking about what God is.

"What does it mean that God is everywhere and everything?" he asked.

"It means that Love is present in all things," I replied.

"So is God in my poop?"

My mind flashed with images of all I'd studied about spirituality: how we disown the Jungian shadow; how we leave our spiritually addictive tendencies only to fly, inflated and ungrounded, into the sun like Icarus; the story of Job and how we accept or deny God. I wanted to tell my son, "Yes, God is everywhere, even in the shit of life . . . *especially* in the shit. If you can find God in the shit, you can find him anywhere."

But I looked at him with the utmost serious expression on my face and simply said, "Yes, God is in your poop. Like I said, God is everywhere."

The sacred is everywhere. If we can stay awake, connected to our Souls, we see that Soul Lessons are some sacred shit.

THE SHIT STORM OF '99

When I was 26 years old and deep in unconscious relationship shit, the universe decided to display this to me with a brilliant and disgusting metaphor.

I was living with my boyfriend, Jonathan, who was managing an apartment building, and many of the units were filled with our friends, including an ex-boyfriend who lived upstairs. There was constant tension and unhealthy communication between us but we all were pretending everything was fine. One Friday night when some friends and I were figuring out what to do, we heard someone running down the hall. All of a sudden, the door flew open. It was my good friend Kari, who lived on the top floor.

"There is *shit* exploding all over the garage!" she screamed.

We all looked at each other in shock, assuming she must be kidding.

"What are you talking about?" Jonathan asked.

"Gallons and gallons of shit are exploding out of pipes, all over cars, in the garage downstairs!" Jonathan and Kari ran down the hall to investigate.

My friend, my ex-boyfriend Sam, and I stood there looking at each other and started laughing. This was ridiculous! Then, suddenly from the toilet we heard, *Glub. Glub.*

We rushed over to the bathroom, where the toilet was quickly filling with a smelly dark-brown substance. We started hysterically yelling and laughing. We looked over and the bathtub had also started to fill. Now the sink was slowly filling up. It was straight out of a horror movie.

"Oh my God!" I screamed. "What do we do?"

"I don't know!" Sam yelled back.

My apartment had just gotten new carpet. All of my belongings were going to be ruined. I went into a mad panic mode.

"Get buckets!" We ran around getting buckets.

"Start bailing!" I screamed.

Kari's boyfriend came down the hall to see what was going on.

"Help us!" I yelled.

"Um, I kinda have a thing . . . about bailing human feces in buckets," was his reply.

"I had that thing until two minutes ago. *Help us!*"

We all began to bail feces in buckets and run it down the hall, dumping it out onto the street. We kept this up at a crazy, disgusting pace while we called 911. The operator hung up on us; I guess she thought the woman screaming, "There is *shit* exploding all over my apartment!" had to be a prank call.

We called the city. They told us to go rent a wet vac. They had no idea that the broken pipe had filled whole cars, via their open sunroofs, with shit. On the first floor, we couldn't open doors of closets and storage rooms because they were so full of sewage.

Eventually the city came and fixed the pipe at the corner of the street that was backing all Seattle's sewage into our tiny apartment building. A team of men in hazmat suits from a private cleanup company came over and began to clean up the disaster. I went to a friend's clean shower and scrubbed myself with soap for over an hour. The photos from that day are totally indescribable.

I am not telling this story for pure shock value, but to really drive home the extreme metaphor that was thrust in my face that day. Often the Soul speaks to us in metaphors through dreams or through fate. It was as if a dream image had sprung to life and I was living a nightmare. With my level of unconsciousness about relationships at the time, my Soul had no other way to reach me. I was an ostrich, head in the sand, choosing denial instead of seeing the unhealthy patterns that were playing out. I later understood that the level of shit in the apartment that day (our apartment got the most shit in the building) matched the level of unconscious-ness in and around me. It was time to get more than a wet vac. So even though my shit storm was literally a shit storm, we all need to look at our lives and trust that God (and meaning) is in the shit.

We are living our own sacred metaphors. We can approach the events and circumstances around us as signposts, messages, and symbols for illumination. Our Souls are calling us to hear them, even when life looks its most dark and bleak.

Divine Shit Storm Soul Journaling

In your journal, start to explore some of your own Divine shit storms by answering the following questions:

1. What are the largest shit storms that have hit my life?

2. Can I view the experiences metaphorically as I would a dream image? What could my Soul have been trying to communicate to me through the unique metaphor of that experience?

3. Because of this specific learning, what do I know deeply and inherently? What am I now, because of my experience, more qualified to understand than any other person on the planet?

Shadow Boxing Inquiry

- Spend some time with your journal and ask your Soul if there are any parts of your shadow that you are currently disowning. Are there any distasteful events, relationships, or parts of your personality in which you feel guilt or shame?

- Next, ask your Soul how you can forgive yourself or if there are any specific actions you need to take to clean up "your side of the street."

CHAPTER 17

CHECKED OUT WITH TRAUMA

"How does one become a butterfly?" she asked pensively. *"You must want to fly so much that you are willing to let go of being a caterpillar."*
—TRINA PAULUS

"God gives us only what we can handle.
Apparently God thinks I'm a badass."
—ANONYMOUS

The Divine shit storms and dark nights we experience in our lives can leave us with a great deal of trauma, which is amazingly effective at disconnecting us from our Souls. In shamanic Soul retrievals, the practitioner locates the missing Soul fragment that is lost in a very literal, energetic way. The traumatic event freezes a piece of Soul, making it impossible to access. After reclaiming the lost piece, we gain access to more of our total vital energy, or *chi*.

Trauma keeps us frozen in the past. Like the Vietnam vet with post-traumatic stress disorder (PTSD) who retells and reexperiences the same story of battle repeatedly, we become tethered to traumatic events from our pasts. The word *trauma* is intense, yet often mild traumas are not even identified as traumatic to the rational mind. Something as simple as being chosen last for the kickball team in fourth grade can be interpreted as "traumatic" by the body—even if our minds write it off and categorize it as a normal part of growing up. These hidden traumas often manifest as messages through dreams at night or through physical symptoms of dissociation such as chills, flightiness, forgetfulness, or spacey feelings that make it difficult to focus.

Sometimes in life we are confronted with major traumas that we need work to heal from: a rape, a war, a robbery, or a serious car accident. Especially in instances of sexual assault or PTSD from living in a war zone, Eye Movement Desensitization and Reprocessing (EMDR) therapy has helped people get relief. Shamanic Soul retrieval done by an experienced and respected clinician is another effective and powerful mode for healing trauma.

Yet all of us face minor traumas and stressors of life that require regular self-care. Many people find Emotional Freedom Techniques (EFT), or tapping, to be an effective way to rewire the synapses in the brain and move the physical body out of a trauma reaction. One of the benefits of EFT is that you can learn the technique and practice on yourself, making it an affordable way to get relief. EFT is great to practice before a big meeting or speech, but it is also used to deal with regular anxiety that builds throughout the day. (See the Resources section at the back of the book for further information on healing trauma.)

In my undergrad psychology program, I remember studying about "learned helplessness." We learned about an experiment where a dog was repeatedly shocked on one side of a cage. The dog (obviously) moved to the other side of the cage to get relief. The experimenters then began shocking the dog on the opposite side of the cage. After finding no escape, eventually the dog would lie down and submit to the shocks. The saddest part of the experiment was that after the experimenters opened the cage door (while continuing the shocks), the dog would stay there in pain instead of getting up to escape. The dog was free to leave the situation yet had already adjusted to his new life of pain.[18] The nature of trauma can send us into depressive self-sabotage that narrows our perception of options and choices. Sometimes in life we have options available to us, such as leaving an abusive relationship or a soul-sucking job, but we stay because of the traumatic reinforcement that has already defeated us.

Some trauma is wired to keep us protected from directly experiencing the traumatic event in the body. When I worked as a counselor at an incest survivors agency, I sat with clients with dissociative identity disorder (known as DID, formerly called multiple personality disorder) as well as clients who were just beginning to experience flashbacks of the sexual assaults from their childhoods. In the first case, the healthy ego had manifested the mental illness to protect the personality from directly experiencing the traumatic event. The others, who were adults when they finally started to remember and experience the trauma, were able to confront the horrific events now because their egos had more coping tools than when they were children experiencing the trauma.

SEEING YOUR TRAUMA

Even the luckiest of us, who have escaped the more challenging aspects of trauma, have some hidden battle wounds. By the nature of being human, we carry traumatic wounds and responses. Because of the traumatic dissociation response, we often do not know consciously when they are activated. This can keep us in an energetic hiding place where we are in mild dissociation and unable to hear the subtle callings of the Soul. The Soul is always trying to get our attention and help us come home, but the loud volume of trauma can make it more challenging to hear Her message of Peace and Love.

One of my clients, Katie, and I noticed that her trauma is triggered whenever the voice of her Soul is calling her to make a move toward authenticity in relation to her family. We call her trauma response "Frank." Frank likes to show up in those important moments when she is about to make a discovery about her family system. Suddenly she becomes very sleepy and begins yawning. She loses the motivation to talk about whatever the issue was. We joke that it feels like very real energetic carbon monoxide poisoning has just taken place. It is as if all the life in her has suddenly become deadened by an energetic gassing. Her trauma is made up of earlier family programming as well as the present-time energies and opinions from her family members. In order to keep her family system intact, her trauma presents itself as an energetic placeholder, keeping her trapped in mundane issues instead of pursuing the developing urgency to address her unfolding empowerment. It is a very real energetic battle with serious ramifications. Who will prevail? Consciousness or unconsciousness? The potential of the ever-changing impulse to life or the controlling predictability of the death wish?

If we are lucky, we begin to notice where our own inner "Franks" show up to hijack our journeys toward our Souls. If appropriate, we work on our trauma through EMDR, EFT, shamanic Soul retrievals, speaking with our Soul in our journals, or some other type of therapy. We begin the important work of gathering our life force back. Once we manage and heal the dissociation, we use the experience from trauma to inform our movement toward wisdom. Trauma then becomes a gift and not solely a holding pattern. We take ownership of our own story and become proactive in our identity. We begin to exude the sense of a life lived on purpose with consciousness while gaining compassion for others along the way.

It is important when beginning to consciously work on trauma that we create safe places to find nurturing and support. A trusted therapist experienced with trauma can be a great support as we navigate the often confusing inner landscape of trauma. It can also be wise to create a list of things that we know will support our self-care during these sensitive times—like a walk in nature, petting a cat, or tea with a good friend. And it is essential to cultivate an inner sanctuary through mindfulness and meditation to soothe ourselves when we notice that we are beginning to dissociate.

To thoroughly discuss trauma would be beyond the scope of this book, as our intentions are only to begin to notice how trauma can derail communication with the Soul. (Again, if trauma is something you have identified as an area that is blocking you from living

Soulfully, please see the Resources section at the back of the book for additional trauma recommendations.) The following two simple exercises are great and approachable ways for anyone to begin to create safety and cultivate self-care.

How to De-Trigger

Sometimes we get triggered or overwhelmed. If you have hit your max and are at the end of your rope, these are two easy things you can do anywhere to calm you back down. These work as mind distractions to derail the stress train. (You can do these anywhere, and they are not obvious. So, if you are in a meeting and begin to feel angry, it is a great place to test them out!)

1. Choose a color and start to search the room for things of that color. For example, if you choose green, see if you can find at least three things in the room that are green. After you find green, you can choose another color.

2. Try to say the alphabet backward in your head. This just takes brainpower and serves as a brief distraction from whatever is raising your blood pressure in the moment, allowing you to de-flood.

Bookending Exercise

When I worked at rehabs with recovering addicts, we identified potential triggers that could, if left unattended, cause a relapse. For example, a client might identify an upcoming wedding where alcohol would be present as a potential trigger. If it was an important wedding to attend (like for a close family member), we would brainstorm "bookends" of support around the event to create structure and accountability to keep them safe. The first bookend would be an activity that would calm them and get them ready for the event. For example, they might go for a calming walk, meditate, or journal about why sobriety was important to them. The second bookend would be an action that would hold them accountable for their behavior, such as a plan to see their sponsor after the wedding. This process was incredibly helpful. The early identification, planning, and accountability all dramatically helped the client be successful while facing stressful situations.

We all have to do things at times that are stressful or expose us to light levels of trauma. It may be going home to visit dysfunctional family for the holidays, working at a soul-sucking job, or attending a particularly stressful meeting. If you are aware that you will be exposing yourself to a stressful Soul-separating situation, bookend the event with Soul reminders and self-loving supports that will help bring you back to yourself.

Safe Place Meditation

You can do this meditation by reading the following or, if you would like a free guided audio version, visit www.ElisaRomeo.com /MeetYourSoul.

Breathe (page 60), Center (page 34), and Ground (page 59). Then imagine yourself walking up a flight of stairs. Each stair is a color of the rainbow; the first is red, the next orange, and then yellow, green, blue, and purple. At the top of the stairs, you walk down a path and encounter your safe place. This place can be a real spot that you love (your favorite beach, garden, or woods) or completely made up. It can be indoors or outdoors. In this safe haven, you may want to imagine a comfy chair, a place to take a nap, or some of your favorite things. You can come here whenever you are feeling overwhelmed. After you leave, follow the path and the stairs back down to your daily life.

CHAPTER 18

FEELING VERSUS EMOTING

"Blues is easy to play, but hard to feel."
—JIMI HENDRIX

"If you've been up all night and cried till you have no more tears left in you—you will know that there comes in the end a sort of quietness. You feel as if nothing was ever going to happen again."
—C. S. LEWIS

To truly connect to the Soul, it is essential to be able to distinguish true feeling from haphazard emoting. Although, to an observer, feeling and emoting can look very similar, they are actually extremely different psychological and spiritual processes. Most people are completely unaware of this crucial distinction that can make a world of difference in healing and connecting to peace in our lives.

It takes courage to truly experience a feeling completely and directly in the body. We often don't give ourselves permission to truly feel our feelings. Instead we suppress, repress, and avoid. But when we truly feel a feeling, we allow our Souls to grow. We squeeze from the body—like toothpaste out of a tube—the heavy weight of previous memories, experiences, and traumas. It can feel as if we are giving birth. When we sit with the feeling, we allow our physical bodies to experience the release. This process is the marriage of the Spirit and the body, the embodiment alchemy, where your ethereal Self is experiencing itself as a body in a body.

When we experience our feelings in this way, we understand that feeling is a powerful form of intelligence. We move beyond how we think we feel to experience a true grounding of identity from the Soul through the body. This is what is known as *embodiment*.

When we emote, it is haphazard, unintentional, and reckless. We are all guilty of emoting at times. But when our identities begin to rely on constant emotive expression, instead of courageously feeling our emotions, we dangerously inhibit Soul connection.

Have you ever been around someone with a flair for dramatics, someone who cries at the drop of a hat? Or maybe you have witnessed someone with an extreme case of sentimentalism? Perhaps you know someone who finds every excuse to become angry and aggressive? In extreme cases, these individuals may have been diagnosed with histrionic personality disorder. They project an air of instability, always on the verge of potential hysteria, as if they've been made raw by emotional sunburn. Instead of having deep strength from within, overemoters create an identity that is dependent on reacting to external situations. Their sense of self is so fragile they do not know who they are outside of their reactivity.

Life for the high emoter is like being trapped in a reactive hell. Because they are attached to the story of their emotional wounds and live as victims, they milk every trauma and drama to maintain their false identity. Releasing the victim story and moving into the true feeling that lies dormant under the emotiveness is extremely challenging and scary. The inner Gremlin uses this fear to keep the ego stuck in a story of conditioned oversensitivity, successfully resisting the opportunity for real healing. Emotions come from our inner Gremlins. Feelings come from Soul.

SERVING THE SOUL

In group therapy or talking circles, participants often unconsciously collude with the Gremlin. If someone begins to cry from an emotive place, it seizes the attention of the group. Not wanting to be insensitive, others rush in to support and validate that person's "feelings." If a group member points out that the display of emotion may be from a habitual place, that person may be accused of insensitivity. In these cases the group has lost its ability to discern between the true release of feelings and Gremlin hijacking.

We do not serve our friends' Souls when we collude with their Gremlins. Sometimes we have to disappoint an ego to empower a Soul connection. If the woman sitting across from you in your women's group has cried this same way for many years on the same topic, she might be stuck in emotionality. If you feel as if you are being repeatedly held hostage, as opposed to witnessing a release, you may be stuck in an enabling and codependent group pattern.

To truly serve the Soul, we must experience real feeling. Feeling clears like a fire. It burns off "story" residue as it merges the ego in the transformative power of the present. When a talking circle experiences a true feeling state, a magic moment captures the room. Time slows and the senses are heightened. This is the experience of sacred space. Feelings from the Soul envelop the group and true transformation occurs. The visible and invisible worlds become one.

The Soul does not reside in the domain of the mind; Her home is in the heart. But because our culture carries an intense head–heart split, we often cannot tell the vast difference between an emotional release and true heart guidance. As you begin to speak to your Soul and work with your Gremlins, you may be unsure of whether you are experiencing a feeling from your Soul or an emotion from your Gremlin. The most powerful way to tell the difference between the two is to directly ask your Soul: *Am I feeling or emoting?*

Awareness is the key to shifting the habit of emotionality. As a daily check-in at addiction treatment centers, clients are commonly given a "feeling chart" and asked to pick three emotions they are experiencing. The chart shows pictures of faces expressing myriad emotions like happiness, sadness, and anger. It is often a challenging exercise. *I feel fat* is not a feeling. *Fine* is not a feeling. Instead clients are encouraged to use feeling words like *happy, frustrated, anxious, desperate, irritated, uncomfortable, disoriented, rageful, blissful,* or even *devastated.* This is a helpful daily practice for all of us, even if it seems simple. Most of us are unaware of our specific feelings throughout the day. Checking in gives us the chance to determine if we need to practice self-care. This is especially key if you were raised in a household where feelings were not understood, identified, or supported. We cannot move toward healing if we are stuck in confusion about our current feeling state. Emotional eating, overworking, and overspending are all attempts to avoid feeling.

A surefire way to tell if you are trapped in emoting is if you are mentally stuck on a topic in an obsessive way. The trappings of the mental plane keep us occupied and busy as we miss our encounter with true feeling transformation. We ruminate to the extent that we are not feeling. But feeling is the way our Souls speak to us. If you allow this powerful Truth to sink in and use this knowledge as a tool for self-transformation, it has the potential to change your entire life.

Feeling Big

When we mentally "spin out," it is often because we are trapped in a cycle of emoting, while the body is searching for a true feeling release. We find ourselves in bed at night going through a laundry list of stresses: *I don't have enough money to pay that bill . . . My boyfriend was such a stubborn ass today . . . I can't believe Janet ignored my phone call . . . I never got to the grocery store to buy the kids cereal for the morning . . .*

If you are ruminating, stop and ask yourself, *What am I avoiding feeling right now?* With this scenario, the feelings will probably be:

overwhelmed, burned out, exhausted, frustrated, and *anxious.* Once you identify your feeling, put one hand on your belly and take some deep breaths. Check your body and notice where you are holding tension and breathe into those places. Set the intention to give yourself permission to feel what you are feeling and then allow your body to fully experience whatever comes up. Allow the feelings to ripple out through your whole body and resonate through all your cells. Pay close attention and breathe as you allow this true body feeling to wash over you. Feel *big.* Try to actually feel the "overwhelm" to its maximum. You may find yourself crying, breathing heavily, or moaning. You may feel heat sensations radiating from your chest. You may feel cold waves down your legs. Resist associating judgment—*this is horrible, I hate this feeling*—and instead just breathe. Stay with this somatic communication as your Soul speaks through your body to your ego.

This is where we find release. We discover that we are intact and stronger on the other side of the feeling wave. We are no longer caught in the white water of emoting. We swim in the vast sea of feeling and emerge holy and wholly renewed.

Transforming Physical Pain

The Soul first whispers, then She speaks, then She screams (often through physical pain) to get our attention. Because of the intense density of the ego, oftentimes only physical messages can get our attention. This meditation will help you to turn toward your Soul if you are experiencing physical pain, so that She can stop yelling and you can transform the physical pain into a feeling.

Sit in meditation with your left hand on your belly. Watch your breath moving up and down and invite your body to speak to you. Put the intention forward that your Soul is going to dialogue with you through your body in Her native language. Locate an area of physical discomfort (headache, stomachache, . . .) in your body and ask your body to translate that physical feeling into an emotional feeling.

Can you find the feeling quality underneath the physical and energetic blockage? Give yourself permission to watch what shows up without judgment. Make a safe place where you allow yourself to truly feel what you feel. You may receive visual images about the issue, or Soul information. This information can be helpful, but watch out for the pull to interpret with your mind or "solve" the problem. The goal is to feel the issue, not fix it. The feeling itself is what will allow for the release and transformation.

CHAPTER 19

SPIRITUAL TEMPER
TANTRUMS

"The experience of the Self is always a defeat for the ego."
—C. G. JUNG

*"For a seed to achieve its greatest expression, it must come
completely undone. The shell cracks, its insides come out and
everything changes. To someone who doesn't understand growth,
it would look like complete destruction."*
—CYNTHIA OCCELLI

"I defy you, stars!"
—ROMEO, FROM WILLIAM SHAKESPEARE'S *ROMEO AND JULIET*

When we experience a Divine shit storm or spin out in emotion, we often feel like the world is against us, and at these times many of us will throw a spiritual temper tantrum (STT). Part of being human is the struggle under the weighty existential question of free will versus fate. We want to feel our power and independence, our ability to shape our existence, but we also want to trust that life supports, nourishes, and sustains us. Because of family conditioning, personality, and life circumstances, some of us are more prone to getting trapped in "why me?" stories than others.

When we are caught in an STT, we feel that God has forgotten us. The universe appears evil, manipulative, and purposeless. Life feels heavy, pointless, and unjust. We identify as Sisyphus, with the never-ending task of pushing the boulder up the mountain for all of eternity. When we are having an STT we are fully immersed in the victim archetype. "Life is doing this *to* me. I have no say, no control, and no escape from the haphazard wheel of fortune that has dealt me a living, hellish nightmare." STTs can go on for days, weeks, years, or, for some, a lifetime or lifetimes.

Yet, when we are in STTs, we are actually closest to our Souls. The reactivity and emotion we feel so strongly in these states is because part of us is well aware that there is another way. In fact, we can *feel* the other way, and that is why we are having such a reaction. We, consciously or unconsciously, feel the potential for life—the potential for Love to split us wide open. We just don't think we are capable of finding the calm eye in the center of the spiritual storm. We sit, paralyzed, unsure how we are going to get through this life test.

The good news is that you do not need to have the answers to "how." You don't need to know how you will trust or how exactly you will reconnect to your Soul. During an STT all you need to do is identify that you are having an STT and remember that *there is another way.* You ask your Soul *Her* opinion on the STT: Why do You think I am having it? Is there a cosmic purpose for what I am going through? What Soul Lesson am I learning? What are two basic steps I can take today to begin to shift this heavy energy? What loving self-care thing can I do to start to feel better? What will bring me a little bit of relief?

Anytime we are caught in an STT, it is because we either cannot hear or are resisting the information from our Soul. There is nothing that She gives us that we can't handle if we are in relationship with Her and with the "why" of it. We need to talk to Her for the "how" of it as well. How do we handle our feelings? What should we do? We need details. Go ahead and ask Her.

For boiling water to turn to steam, the temperature needs to get hot enough. If we continue to lift the lid to check the temperature of the water, we are going to have to wait longer than if we hold tight and keep the lid on. If we can endure and understand during an STT that our Soul temperature is rising for the necessary process of alchemical transformation, we can have more patience for the process.

Stopping an STT in Its Tracks

Next time you begin to spiritually boil, remember: We don't need to know how we will trust or how we will reconnect to our Souls. During an STT, all we need to do is identify that we are having one, and then remember that there is another way. If you are in an STT, ask your Soul Her opinion on the STT. Some questions for inquiry are the following:

- Why do You think I am having it?

- Is there a cosmic purpose for what I am going through?

- What Soul Lesson am I learning?

- What are the most common ways I react when I am having an STT (overeating, avoidance, addictive relationships, . . .)? Am I doing any of that now?

After you are done inquiring about your STT, ask your Soul the following:

- What are two basic steps I can take today to begin to shift this heavy energy?

- What loving self-care thing can I do to start to feel better?

- What will bring me a little bit of relief?

Choose one of your small, measurable action steps toward relief and think of a small reward to motivate you, which you will give to yourself (a bath, a walk, . . .) after you complete it. Follow through on your plan.

CHAPTER 20

SPIRALING OUT

"The ultimate weakness of violence is that it is a descending spiral, begetting the very thing it seeks to destroy."
—DR. MARTIN LUTHER KING, JR.

"The spiral is a spiritualized circle. In the spiral form, the circle, uncoiled, unwound, has ceased to be vicious; it has been set free."
—VLADIMIR NABOKOV

We know that the Soul orchestrates what happens in our lives, and how we react to this orchestration is spurred by the constant battle between the life wish and the death wish. Energy naturally builds on itself and gains momentum. Because of this reality, when we lose this battle, it unfortunately often ends with us addictively spiraling out from our true nature. Learning about this dynamic can help us to recognize it and stop the cycle.

Our natural life wish is imbued with the sacred. When we are connected to something greater than ourselves, when we're thankful, when we're humbled by the Divine, we act within the impulses of our true and highest Self. When we are naturally ourselves, we are naturally spiritual, whether we consciously identify with the term or not. In this state, life has meaning and purpose. When we are in death wish, we are separated from the sacred, cast aside, and forgotten, like motherless children, set adrift in a sea of nothingness.

In her phenomenal book *Addiction to Perfection,* Jungian analyst Marion Woodman explains the negative death wish as a
spiral, "a hurricane swirling its victim headlong into unconsciousness. The natural spiritual hunger, if it is not fed by the sacred, is
trapped in the demonic."[19] The spiral spins toward unconsciousness, resulting in addictive behaviors or, if accelerated, a full-
blown addiction.

The spiral is an incredibly helpful symbol to visualize how energy gains momentum in our constant life wish–death wish battle. An image commonly found in nature, the spiral appears as the
inherent pattern in a nautilus shell, the spin of a DNA helix, or the
massive spiral we reside within—the galaxy itself. The death wish
spiral aims to hypnotize, numb out, and dumb the senses. "You
are getting sleepy . . ." are the words from the classic hypnotists, as
the clichéd cartoon character's eyes turn into rotating spirals. We
hear common phrases like: "I spiraled into addiction" or "I was in
a self-hatred spiral."

But spiraling is not solely negative; we can also spiral in the direction of radical self-love. As Woodman notes: "My central image
is a spiral, which can move two ways: out toward release or in
toward destruction."[20]

We can spiral up and we can spiral down—we can spiral in
and spiral out. We act with courage and love toward ourselves and
it begins to build on itself. Like a hurricane gaining momentum
or a snowball gaining size as it rolls downhill, we can utilize the
energy of the spiral for our Highest Good.

Our choice for whether we spiral up or down always begins with a single impulse. The impulse then either gains momentum or is halted through the next immediate choice we make. We can always change direction—no matter where we are in the spiral— but we have a small window of opportunity to easily identify and shift negative spiraling. It's much more difficult to hold your power against a full-blown hurricane than a small gust of wind. Yet, for most of us, at some point in our lives, facing a full-blown hurricane is inevitable. It is often part of the Soul's plan to grow us into our true selves by choosing life when we can only feel death surrounding us.

There is a Cherokee legend that beautifully sums up the essence of our spiraling struggle:

> An old Cherokee man was teaching his grandson about life. "A fight is going on inside me," he said to the boy. "It is a terrible fight, and it is between two wolves. One is evil—he is anger, envy, sorrow, regret, greed, arrogance, self-pity, guilt, resentment, inferiority, lies, false pride, superiority, and ego. The other is good—he is joy, peace, love, hope, serenity, humility, kindness, benevolence, empathy, generosity, truth, compassion, and faith. The same fight is going on inside you—and inside every other person, too."
>
> The grandson thought about this for a minute and then asked his grandfather, "Which wolf will win?"
>
> The old Cherokee simply replied, "The one you feed."

It is the sign of true maturity and wisdom to identify spiraling in our lives in the present moment and then shift conditions (much like the weather) rather than identify as the spiral itself. In this way we can, for example, feel depression but not *be* the depression. It is this subtle but powerful shift of identity that makes even the biggest storms manageable.

When we spiral toward life wish, we catapult into the vortex of Soul. When we spiral toward death wish, the result is Soul loss. (Of course, we never *actually* lose our Soul, but we *can* lose our connection to Her. And because our connection is the ego's *whole* understanding and interpretation of Soul, this sometimes tentative and elusive connection is, very much, everything.)

Which Wolf Are You Feeding?

The wolf that we feed is the wolf that wins. This inquiry brings to light the unconscious life wish–death wish battle, which is always occurring. Answer the following questions in your journal:

1. What is your biggest "death wolf" (overeating, shopping, anorexia, procrastination, perfectionism, depression)?

2. How and when does your wolf show up? (When you are stressed? Lonely? Tired? After a visit with family?)

3. What do you feed your wolf (food, things, self-hate)?

4. What are some alternative healthy actions you can take when you are tempted to feed your inner addictive wolf (yoga, meditation, a nice bath, a walk)?

Spiraling Thoughts and Actions

This exercise brings awareness to the behaviors and thoughts that occur when you spiral—both negatively and positively. Love spirals us up; fear spirals us down.

In your journal, create four spirals. For the first spiral, write out the common thoughts you have when you are in a negative death wish spiral. (If you would like for an added visual, you can actually write your words in the shape of the spirals as you do this exercise.)

For the second, note the common actions/behaviors that occur when you have those types of thoughts. After you complete the negative spirals, investigate how you spiral in positive ways. First write out the thoughts that are characteristic of positive, life-affirming spiraling and then write the actions you take when you are in that positive energy of life wish.

CHAPTER 21

WHO'S TO JUDGE?

"Don't let the noise of others' opinions drown out your own inner voice."
—STEVE JOBS

"When people show you who they are, believe them."
—MAYA ANGELOU

"Just trust yourself, then you will know how to live."
—JOHANN WOLFGANG VON GOETHE

Another hurdle people often face as they begin to hear their Souls is distaste toward the direct and opinionated nature in which the Soul can speak. Sometimes when we feel our Soul's Truth, it can feel to the ego as though we are being judgmental. And many of us have a strong negative association with the idea of judgment. We may be assaulted with images of reactive daytime courtroom shows that are big on "tellin' it like it is" in a state of power-fed tyranny. For most of us, spirituality has no room for judgment. We often consider compassion, kindness, and unconditional love to be the essential spiritual traits. We picture the gentleness of the Dalai Lama, the pacifism of Gandhi, or the unconditional love of Jesus or the Buddha. Most of us do not consider it in any way spiritual to be *judgmental.*

Yet the Soul is attached. She is opinionated and knows what your specific mission is in your lifetime, and She cares if you achieve it. The Soul does not judge from a place of fear, separation, or division, but from the calm, clear knowing of Divine judgment. *Soul judgment is extremely different from ego judgment.* Soul judgment never comes from an attempt to prove, divide, or conquer. It is not greedy with power or hungry for control; instead, it points us in the direction of the Love that humankind and the planet desperately need at this time.

Gandhi's Soul mission was to display pure pacifism to the planet. He was successful in achieving his mission. Yet it could also be said that Frederick Douglass, the black abolitionist who advocated for African American troops to enlist in the Civil War, was successful in his Soul mission as well. If Douglass had minimized his Soul by comparing himself with Gandhi, we might never have had Douglass's form of Love on the planet. There are diverse ways that different Souls want to love. To know if we are personally aligned with our spiritual mission, we must directly ask the Soul. To hear the answer, we need to be clear of egoic judgment about what that mission may be.

This ability comes from spiritual sight, where we are accepting of reality and given permission to truly see what is before us. An example of this would be when Jesus overturned the moneylenders' tables outside the temple. He did not react with a Big Lebowski "it's all good" form of Love but with strong passion, direction, and guidance from the fierce Love of attachment. This type of Love is decidedly *here* and cares about what happens. This Love burns away any residue or sediment that blocks true spiritual sight.

This distaste for judgment is often so strong in our puritanical society that it manifests as a reactionary, supercharged, "it's all good" New Ager attitude in mainstream spiritual circles. This prevalent shadow toward judgment is a by-product of the early stages of spiritual development that our culture is in. We do not have the spiritual maturity to understand that Soul judgment is not anti-Love; rather, it comes directly from Love.

This cultural desire to be seen as spiritually compassionate often clouds our abilities to discern what is actually right for the Soul. In the quest to "turn the other cheek," we are paradoxically judging ourselves for judgment itself, and sometimes for merely having opinions. The result of this aversion fosters repression of our gut feelings and instincts from Soul as we second-guess ourselves and ostracize intuition. When fear of judgment diminishes our intuition, we have a problem.

While working on a suicide hotline, I had a powerful experience that displayed my own resistance toward Soul judgment, which, besides dulling my natural instincts, could have potentially put me in danger.

"Hello," said the voice on the other end of the line.

I felt immediate disgust run through my body.

My ego felt shocked and appalled by my reaction. Here was a person reaching out, calling a suicide crisis line to get help, and I was having a judgmental reaction.

He began to talk about the issues that he was facing in his life. He was in a loveless marriage and his wife was emotionally abusive to him. I was compassionate with his story, and I decided my initial reaction was way off the mark. This man was kind, sad, and reaching out for help.

Then he began talking about the sexual issues in his marriage. He felt so lonely and unlovable. He started talking about the details of his sexual relationship with his wife, and then he changed the focus to me.

"How do you feel about sex?" he asked.

I sat in stunned silence, not sure what was happening.

"Tell me about what you like in bed," he continued, and then he quickly segued into a detailed description of his penis.

I hung up the phone feeling disgusted. He'd used my naive compassion to take advantage of me. Even though nothing happened physically, I felt victimized. I stood up and walked over to my co-workers and told them the story.

"Oh, yeah, you talked to Sicko Sam. He calls every few months hoping to get some fresh meat that doesn't know his game."

How is it that after hearing only the way he said "Hello," my intuition, my Soul, knew immediately who this man was? There was absolutely nothing on a rational level that had given me that sign. His "Hello" did not seem like it was uttered in a perverted or particularly seedy way. Yet my Soul knew immediately. My Soul wanted to hang up the phone as soon as I heard his voice.

I realized I did not want this resistance to judgment, this over-identification I had with being a "compassionate" and "loving" person, to separate me from my instincts, which could keep me safe. I was grateful that this all took place over the safety of a phone line; in person, the results could have been far more dangerous.

The point of Divine judgment is not to foster separation but to connect us to Truth as we sweep away cobwebs of illusion. Would you be judging a tiger if you called it dangerous? Tigers are wild animals that very well could rip your head off. This may seem like a ridiculous example, but people are psychologically doing this constantly. They put themselves in front of an energetic tiger (like an emotionally abusive person), get their asses kicked, and then are confused about why the pretty kitty had an attitude.

The crux of the issue lies in the fact that the compassionate, sympathetic seeker feels the pain of the perpetrator so strongly. Empathic, sensitive, clairsentient people are especially at risk of doing this. They energetically see and feel the traumas, dramas, and challenges the perpetrator faces. Then they match his energy. Their intuition has them literally feeling how the other person feels while losing their own reality. This is what I refer to as energetic codependency.[21] Energetic codependency feeds on the motto "How I feel depends on how you feel." In exchange for acceptance and approval, they lose the ability to see clearly. (To find information about my book *Authentic Intuition* on this topic, see the Resources section.)

EMBRACING FIERCE LOVE

Our society does not show us many models of fierce Love. Instead, we are bombarded in our media with relationships riddled with the surface emotionality of a Hallmark card—codependent and unimaginative. Then, because of the avoidance of truth in relationships, our Souls seek to find a sense of ourselves in other ways.

When I worked at an incest survivor agency, I remember a client discussing her struggle around the holidays. Within the previous year she had begun having flashbacks of nightly rapings from her father during her childhood. She confronted her family with her memories, but they would not accept her Truth. Her father was a dentist, a soccer coach, a pillar of the community. She must just be mistaken, and she was probably crazy.

She was extremely wounded and fragile. With little support and reflection, she verged on the defeated acceptance that maybe she was, indeed, mistaken. With the holidays coming up, she wanted to go home, back to the house where the rape had occurred, and join in the act of pretending the family had no shadows. She told me that in the spirit of Christmas, she should be like Jesus and "turn the other cheek."

Many religious individuals carry the common misunderstanding that Jesus was passive. Never confuse his love with the softness that results from avoidance. Whether you believe in Jesus or not, Christianity has a huge effect on our heavily Christian culture, which influences our collective psychology.

I think Jesus might have marched back to the house of her father in a state of fierce grace. With no denial of the Truth, he would confront the situation and allow Love to stream through him, regardless. He would not allow his ego to block the Love of the universe, but he would also not deny the darkness present. You cannot heal what you do not choose to see. Repression and denial will never move us out of the dark.

I was always bothered by the trend to wear "Love Sees No Color" T-shirts. Love sees color. Love *made* color. Love *is* color. And Love loves, regardless of color. That doesn't mean She doesn't see it. I understand the intended message of the T-shirt, which is that Love does not discriminate. It may feel as if I am being picky with wording, getting caught in semantics, but this wording reflects to me exactly *why* we are not able to move beyond discrimination in our culture. It feels to me that we sorely underestimate Love if we think we need to become blind to be held by Her gaze. Love is not color-blind. Love is powerful 20/20 sight noticing the minute differences within the color spectrum as well as all forms of diversity. We do not get there by avoidance, denial, or blurring our unique attributes, talents, and gifts. Love is the fierce focus of consciousness. We are being called not to deny but to love more fully.

The energy of the Divine feminine, which appears in a fierce form as Kali, the Goddess of Destruction, is able to distinguish flaws in character with Her impeccable sight; then, with intent to heal, She confronts the wounds with fire. There is no room for squirming. Her gaze will never lie to Her or another. She is undoubtedly trustable. Where our ego selves would run, She commands us to stay. And stay we will! In Her gaze there is no other option.

We also need to be realistic with what we can contain and maintain energetically. Just because we understand these things intellectually does not mean that we are energetically and spiritually at that phase of development. There is wisdom in knowing how and when to choose battles. My client was nowhere near psychologically and emotionally equipped to face her perpetrator father that Christmas. We can learn from our models, but we also need to listen to the voices of our Souls so that we are not marching our psychological health into the den of the lion. We cannot tame the beast without a few lessons in lion taming.

The other day, as I was working with a client, it became very apparent that her avoidance of judgment was keeping her trapped in unconscious roles with unhealthy people in her life who acted like energetic vampires. When I asked her how she felt around a specific person she told me, "I feel exhausted afterward; I feel sick." She had been denying her energetic truth because, as she said, "I didn't want to be all judge-y."

Don't deny your Soul's Truth for fear of being considered judgmental. As opposed to the clean vision of Spirit, the Soul is filled with opinions, feelings, and Divine judgments. This is because the Soul has a specific agenda for your life and needs to be able to translate that information to the ego.

When we judge with spiritual awareness, it is called discernment. Success in our ability to discern lies in our honest assessment of where we are in our spiritual development. We must be well practiced in the art of allowing the fierce feminine to burn away the remnants of ego before we face perpetrators, energetic vampires, or the harsh critics in our lives. Sometimes we need to choose to protect the small seedlings of our Souls before planting them in the direct path of an emotional tornado. The storm threatens to uproot our very real and hard-won work toward growth. This type of protection is truly loving of the Self. It is not weak or avoidant; it is a powerful move toward acquiring the necessary trait of discernment.

Judge the Judger

It's time to explore your relationship with judgment. Grab your journal and start writing. Is there any place in your life where you have been avoiding your intuitive truth for fear of being seen as judgmental? Are you able to see Divine judgment as spiritual, or do you have a belief that judgment is always unevolved?

Storm of Judgment

This exercise is for those times when you have quieted your voice and allowed a fear of judgment to block your Soul Truth. Like with brainstorming, do not monitor, censor, or critique your ideas; this will keep the flow open. With Storm of Judgment, focus on a topic where you feel you have experienced a loss of voice (maybe at a recent meeting or with a family member). Your page is a safe place to judge right now. (After the exercise, you may want to rip it up or burn it.) Get into a judgment mind-set and, without stopping your pen, write for at least a full page about what has been upsetting you. When you are done, read over your page and assess which judgments feel like they are from ego and which feel like your Soul's opinion. You may want to transfer the notes from your Soul into another journal for future reference.

If you are feeling heated at the end of the exercise, be sure to take some breaths and talk to your Soul about what calming or action steps you can take to improve the situation.

CHAPTER 22

WHO, ME? CLAIMING SPIRITUAL AUTHORITY

"If I speak in the tongues of men and of angels,
but have not love, I am a noisy gong or a clanging cymbal.
And if I have prophetic powers, and understand all mysteries
and all knowledge, and if I have all faith, so as to remove mountains,
but have not love, I am nothing. If I give away all I have, and if I
deliver up my body to be burned, but have not love, I gain nothing."
—I CORINTHIANS 13:1–13

"In choosing your god, you choose your way of looking at the universe.
There are plenty of gods . . . The god you worship is the god you deserve."
—JOSEPH CAMPBELL

The final block that we will address is one of the most crucial to overcome in order to claim our spiritual power. Many of us were raised in paradigms where we were taught to look outside ourselves to connect to the Divine. Whether raised in a strictly religious home, a decidedly atheistic environment, or a house where spiritual questions were avoided and ignored, most of us were not encouraged to look within to find answers. Without inner Soul knowing, we are subject to the waves of cultural bias, power-based control executed from others while divorced from our own spiritual authority. Many of us were raised looking up to a man in a pulpit interpreting the "word of God" from a book for us. We learned from our parents, who brought us to hear the man, that the man reading had the answers. Wanting to be good children, we obliged, understanding full well that our beliefs must be approved by our first external spiritual authorities—the most powerful figures in the household, our parents. Our parents are the first individual faces where we project God and Goddess. Rife with all the human complications found within the parent–child relationship, spiritual development comes when we begin to do the work of detangling the massive God projection in order to reveal our inner God and Goddess.

Of course, families do exist who belong to a religious community while also encouraging their children's inner spiritual connection. Yet, for the most part, we as a society have misplaced our Divine birthright of confidence with extremely low spiritual self-esteem. The effort it takes to become spiritually self-aware often takes a backseat to the busyness of our days. The developmental stages of spirituality are frequently not taken into consideration as we view each other through thick lenses of programmed beliefs, reactions, and misunderstandings.

We have developed a "little old me?" attitude toward the most primary relationship—the relationship with the Divine. Instead of trusting our own inner spiritual experiences, we look around for others to do the heavy lifting. We can't believe that we are deserving enough to claim and know our own deep spiritual truths. The question "If not you, who?" is particularly relevant on the spiritual path. No one else can know your Soul the way you can. The dominant religious history says that God is out there, up there, over there, through there. Yet God is available right now, right here, for you—through the Divine interpretation of your Soul.

If everything is made from God, by God, how could we not be a part of God, ultimately, at our essential creative root? When we can understand and feel our hearts, we do not need proof of miracles to know God or meaning.

Don't hand your spiritual authority to "experts." Eventually, we will all know the answers to our own inner questions regarding spirit. It may be on our deathbeds, after we cross over, or while we are waiting to unveil consciously in another lifetime. There is little else to do but turn toward and discover the real Truth of who you are and why you are here.

This direct knowing is known as *gnosis*. Gnosis is a form of knowledge, a way in which we know. Instead of understanding through information, other outside experts, other people's stories, or factual information, gnosis is about having a *direct relationship* with the Soul. If our world relied on this type of knowing for spiritual understanding, wars of religion, belief, or opinion would quickly become extinct. This is because when we know something directly, we lose interest in power. As consciousness heals, we in turn lose the desire to convert, control, or convince. We become content with our own personal experience of knowing and lose the appetite for the "rightness" of our beliefs.

Even in the New Age culture, the avoidance of spiritual ownership is rampant. Caroline Myss says in her brilliant book *Entering the Castle*: "The 'new age' isn't new any longer. It's middle-aged and needs a makeover."[22] I have witnessed many tyrannical and oppressive "Love and Light-ers" carrying a wicked shadow over them. Though they are armed with a list of "loving beliefs," the energy they emit is still separatist, one-sided, and undeveloped. Of course, there are many self-described "light workers" deeply nourished by their own spiritual well, not interested in oppressing others with an invisible and silent standard of "light" tyranny. But unintegrated, unexamined, and unchallenged "Love" can be just as fundamentalist as any fear-based God.

I recently took my son to *The Lego Movie*. The hilarious character of Unikitty is a perfect example of the New Age character I'm talking about. Unikitty is a sweet and adorable cuddly pink kitty—complete with a mystical unicorn horn. While welcoming her new friends to her home of Cloud Cuckoo Land, she introduces her hometown: "Here in Cloud Cuckoo Land, there are no rules! There's no government, no babysitters, no bedtimes, no frowny faces, no bushy mustaches, and no negativity of any kind." To which the black-wearing and edgy Wyldstyle character sarcastically retorts: "You just said the word *no*, like one thousand times." Unikitty continues: "And there's also no consistency . . . Any idea is a good idea, except the *not* happy ones." As she finishes her fundamentalist positivity speech, she morphs into a red angry monster kitty and her voice becomes dark and evil: "Those you push down deep inside where you never, ever, ever, *ever* find them."[23] Unikitty exemplifies unintegrated and unexamined spirituality—as we cling to the tyrannical light, the shadow looms large, waiting for an opportunity to attack. When we trade our authenticity for the *ideas* of what we think spirituality should look like, we only create more ego.

I've worked personally with talented healers, capable of psychically assessing and healing others' medical mysteries yet controlled by a wicked, power-hungry, and inflated egoic shadow. What appears to us as a miracle may very well be mired with agendaed intention behind it. We are so spiritually starved that when we see proof of miracles, we immediately assume the miracle worker is in direct and favored connection to God. Miracles do not necessarily equate with "proof of Love." Miracles can come purely from a result of understanding certain laws of the universe, in other words, glorified spiritual magic tricks. This spiritual sleight of hand can distract us from the real question: is this practitioner interested in power or is he working from the heart? This can be very difficult to sort out because if practitioners are unconscious about their motivations at all, they may be lying to themselves as well. Hoodoo, voodoo, miracles, psychic prowess, proof of levitation, or telekinesis does not *in and of itself* prove spiritual evolution.

The temptation to fall for this type of miracle magic comes from our own separation, forgetfulness, and misunderstanding of our Godliness. This is, of course, not the deluded misinterpretation of our ego as God, but as our source Self, our Spirit Self, our Soul Self as the great piece of Divinity that it is.

OTHER GUIDING VOICES

Besides claiming our spiritual authority with spiritual teachers and healers, we also need to stay spiritually awake with the spirits themselves. Many clients come to me in search of connecting to their spirit guides or to spirits that have crossed over. I ask them if they have a strong connection with their Souls—one where they can hear information in order to make decisions. If they do not, we first work to connect to their Souls before speaking with their guides.

At times clients say, "I am not sure I hear my Soul, but I can hear my spirit guide. Is that the same thing?" The answer to this question is, "Absolutely not." If you are working directly with spirit guides, archangels, or other beings without bodies, it is essential that you first have a strong relationship with and ability to hear your Soul.

It is often surprising to people to discover that we are able to hire and fire our spirit guides. Spirit guides can be incredibly helpful, but sometimes our Souls direct us to move on from specific guides. This can be both shocking and empowering.

The reason it can be shocking is because many of us assume that an entity identifying as an angel or spirit guide must have incredible wisdom and potentially know what is better for us than we could . . . after all, it is an angel! And although they may know more than your ego what is best for you, they never know better than your Soul.

I am a trans-medium, meaning that I have the ability to channel other entities, yet I choose not to. When I speak to spirits on the other side, I speak with them directly but do not give them permission to come into my body. What I have come to find is that the beings of the light are usually not interested in entering your body as a means to give you information. True light beings recognize your Soul's sovereignty; they trust your Soul enough to not want to "take over" and intrude. If you have ever witnessed a true trans-medium channeling for a group, they typically say, "Hello!" and then immediately vacate the body to allow the other entity to "come in" and "take over." This says a lot about the level of respect given to the personality and body of the channel the "enlightened" Soul has used.

You chose your unique personality and incarnated in your body at this time for a reason. Beings without bodies who respect the Soul's journey understand the importance of what you are learning and do not infringe on your right to be here.

If you are a trans-medium, I seriously urge you to develop a strong and clear relationship with your Soul, and ask Her opinion on who, when, where, and why you channel, if you channel entities through your body. I can't even begin to tell you how many well-intentioned channelers I have worked with who have been manipulated and controlled by beings without bodies, their Souls hijacked in exchange for a "flashy channeling show." The temptation arises from the reality that these entities often have some relevant and insightful information that appears helpful and in service of the light. Yet, when you challenge these entities or try to break the "channeling contract," prepare to get energetically attacked with fatigue, headaches, or dissociative symptoms like confusion or memory loss. The focus should be less about the information coming from the channeling and more about the energy in which the channeling is being done.

I often hear clients speak of a book, poem, or message that is channeled by another entity as being somehow inherently "better." I am not sure where this trend started. Just as there are angry humans controlled by their misguided and illusionary belief that they are separate from Source, there are also unevolved spirits, angrily trying to reclaim their relationship with God. In plain terms, what that means is that I often view channeled material with more, not less, skepticism. Just because you don't have an ass doesn't mean you aren't one.

I have witnessed spirits who present themselves to me as incredible angelic beings, bright white and gold, emanating light with full wings. Yet when questioned about their true nature (which I always do immediately) or asked to leave, they become nasty and attacking. Spirits can shape-shift their appearance. These masquerading entities present as Love and light but are full of agenda for power and control. Some of these beings even perform convincing "miracles" through the humans they have tricked. What appears on the surface as a loving healing may have behind it a contract for these dark entities to use the "healed" as host. If we pray to these entities and give them our power, they receive an energy "hit." It can become complicated, because some beings, just like humans, *believe themselves to be* in service of the light when they have their own limited views.

If we cannot hear our Souls, we have no ability to really tell who is actually before us. They say that the devil always speaks in half-truths, meaning fakers use the light to disguise the dark. This is why discernment is essential when working with beings without bodies. (Although it's also helpful to be able to discern this with humans!)

The spiritual path is incredibly challenging to navigate. It is remarkably easy to get inflated, deflated, and lost along the path through the subtle realms. It is the constant testing that comes from being human. As we sign up to "come down and forget," we also have the opportunity to "come down and remember," to rejoin with our Soul through the experience of the testing itself. This conscious and joyful experiencing of humanity and Divinity is the joyful reunion of body, Soul, and Spirit.

Once you know your Soul, you are never again subject to give your authority away. You own your truth directly and with certainty. You are no longer at risk of trading your heart's knowing for another, more flashy convincing argument. Slickly packaged "experts" and even well-intended advice are now subject to direct and loving scrutiny by your Soul. You are finally free to rest at your home within yourself.

If Not You, Who?

It's time to journal again. Ask your Soul Her opinion about your spiritual self-esteem. Here are some questions to get you thinking:

- How much do you own your direct connection to your Soul?

- Are you relying on other intermediaries?

- How healthy is your spiritual self-esteem?

- Do you have any spirit guides you work with regularly? Is there anything you need to know to work with them in a way that honors your Soul's role as the boss?

Trusting Your Inner Guru

Are there any spiritual teachers or beliefs that have been making your Soul seem wrong? Do you have any spiritual "shoulds" that might piss off your Soul? Ask Her opinion about your current practices and teachers and get Her opinion about whether they fit into the plan She has for you. Remember, although well intentioned, many spiritual teachers forget this important element of the Soul's plan. Also ask your Soul about timing. A practice or teacher may have been great for you in the past, but maybe you have outgrown them. Or, although talented, maybe the healer, teacher, or program is better timed for the future and not now. Ask Her to find out.

Sacred Soul Ceremony

Hold a sacred Soul ceremony for you and your Soul. See this as a way to make conscious your new relationship with Her. Talk to Her and ask what's the best way to consecrate the relationship. She may want you to find a ring She loves and hold a wedding ceremony complete with Soul vows. This may be witnessed by close friends or held completely alone between you and your Soul.

She may want you to have a physical reminder of Her on your body, initiated by a tattoo. Be sure to ask Her what image she feels most represents Her and will remind you that She is always there for guidance and support.

Whatever you decide, hold your ceremony with the care, reverence, and respect this holy relationship deserves.

PART IV

CLAIMING YOUR SOUL LIFE

CHAPTER 23

So . . . What's My Purpose?

"When we give in the world what we want the most,
we heal the broken part inside each of us."
—Eve Ensler

"Ultimately, man should not ask what the meaning of his life is, but
rather he must recognize that it is he who is asked. In a word, each man
is questioned by life; and he can only answer to life by answering for his
own life; to life he can only respond by being responsible."
—Viktor Frankl

"Follow your passion, stay true to yourself, never follow someone
else's path. (Unless you're in the woods and you're lost and you
see a path—then by all means you should follow that.)"
—Ellen DeGeneres

Now that you've learned how to get in touch with your Soul and how to overcome some of the most common blocks to clear communication, it's time to find out why you are here. Let's get down to the good stuff—figuring out your purpose.

Your purpose is to embody your Soul on Earth. This is much less about *what* and much more about *how*. Many people become lost searching for the *thing* that they are supposed to do. Your purpose is not to write a book, work at a homeless shelter, or star in a musical on Broadway. The Soul may *use* those things as motivation to help you to embody your true nature, but do not mistake the "finger pointing at the moon" for the moon itself. Many people confuse the reward with the ultimate goal. This is why so many people still feel empty and lost when they finally achieve their "dream." I speak with many clients who are confused by this phenomenon, but it's a very common and extremely painful mistake.

The Soul Journey is not measured through external facts and accomplishments but *by the energy that we emit along our path.* You cannot be spiritually successful if you are famous and demeaning. You also cannot be spiritually successful if you spend all your time serving the world by helping others if it is not truly Soul directed. If it doesn't come from Soul, it is ultimately not serving. I frequently see people enact concepts of what it is to be spiritual (volunteering at a shelter or donating money to a good cause), yet they are enacting these actions from their mind, their brain, from an idea that their ego has deemed "good."

The world is in a state of planetary chaos and needs serious care and attention. I am not suggesting that actions are unnecessary or that we use Soul as an excuse to lounge in denial or spiritual narcissism. The world needs action. But the world does not need your guilty servitude.

We do not find our Souls by copying other "spiritual people" or "spiritual rules" or by forcing ourselves to enact concepts of what our egos *believe* to be spiritual. Soul Work is not intellectual. While these "good" actions may temporarily help others, if we are not connected to the energy of the Soul, life remains conceptual instead of embodied and alive. Besides causing health problems, this can cause spiritual problems. The Soul does not give up and go away. She will continue to try and bring you to Her. The journey *is the goal,* and the goal is to break open to the energy and the experience of the unique flavor of Love that you are.

This is why, in and of itself, it is not spiritual to recycle, become a vegetarian, do yoga, or chant. We all have met some angry environmentalists, perfectionistic yogis, and fundamentalist raw foodies. Your spiritual identity is not about keeping a "goodness" tally on a scorecard; it is about surrendering to the truth of who you are. You, specifically. We need you. Again, it is not about what you are doing; it is how you are doing it.

You can trust your passions and your instincts. Who you are as a personality is perfectly chosen by the Soul. Your Soul may want you to help raise planetary consciousness by teaching salsa, playing with pebbles on the beach on Saturdays, becoming an expert figure skater, or volunteering at a homeless shelter. The trick is to ask and hear your specific Soul's marching orders. Then the "what" becomes the "how" as you enjoy the marriage of external action with internal Soul illumination. You learn to be guided by Soul feeling and heart-navigation.

Heaven on Earth: Your Soul Mission Statement

We can have heaven on Earth now. This exercise will give you clarity on what your Soul actually needs to be fulfilled. It is not about the details of the "what" (I will become a vet) but about identifying the "why" (I want to be of service, protect, and heal). Don't worry—we'll cover more on the "what" and "how" in the next chapter.

As it is for any powerful organization or company, creating a mission statement can be incredibly helpful. When you identify your Soul's values and discern the qualities and feelings that your Soul needs to be fulfilled, it helps bring clarity to all the decisions you face in life.

So grab your journal and work through the steps that follow to identify one clear, concise, simple sentence that encompasses your Soul mission statement. Make it easily memorable, so you can remind yourself often of what you are *really* here to do.

Step I: First, set the stage to receive some big Soul information. Set the intention to get information from your Soul about who you actually are on a Soul level. In a private and quiet place, breathe (page 60), center (page 34), and ground (page 59).

Step 2: To warm up, write the phrase *Who am I?* on the top of the page.

Step 3: Without editing, respond with the first thought that comes to your head. Jot it down. Continue to ask yourself the question and write your different responses down the page. Try not to judge yourself and avoid labeling your answers as good or bad. You may need to do this up to 50 times to go beyond surface answers and begin to unveil the deeper layers of who your Soul is. Some of the answers might bring up emotions. Breathe and keep writing until you feel fully "done."

Step 4: Look over the list and note any themes that appeared.

Step 5: Next, peruse the list of Soul actions (or verbs) below and ask your Soul to choose two to four options that call to Her or stand out in some way. (These are just to get you thinking, so feel free to add new verbs that are not on the list, if others come to you.)

- Soul Actions: Adapt, Appreciate, Believe, Build, Catalyze, Categorize, Cause, Coach, Communicate, Connect, Construct, Contribute, Create, Dance, Defend, Design, Discern, Discover, Educate, Encourage, Enlighten, Entertain, Envision, Explore, Facilitate, Guide, Heal, Identify, Impact, Implement, Improve, Inspire, Integrate, Lead, Measure, Organize, Paint, Plan, Protect, Provide, Relate, Serve, Sing, Support, Teach, Translate, Uplift, Use, Write

Step 6: Next is a list of common Soul values to get you started. (Again, if others come to you, jot them down.) Pick three to six that most deeply resonate and write them in your journal.

- Soul Values: Abundance, Acceptance, Adventure, Altruism, Amusement, Awareness, Beauty, Comfort, Compassion, Connection, Consciousness, Creativity, Daring, Depth, Devotion, Empathy, Flexibility, Freedom, Grace, Gratitude, Happiness, Health, Imagination, Integrity, Intelligence, Intimacy, Joy, Justice, Kindness, Love, Loyalty, Meaning, Nurture, Partnership, Passion, Peace, Play, Pleasure, Presence, Radiance, Security, Sensuality, Strength, Success, Surrender, Tranquility, Vision, Wisdom

Step 7: Play around with all the words She chose and write out different combinations of potential Soul mission statements in your journal. Have fun with it. Use the template below as an example to get your creative juices flowing: "My Soul's mission is to Soul Action, Soul Action, and Soul Action to create Soul Value."

For example, my Soul's mission is to motivate, educate, and inspire to create connection to Soul. Try using anywhere from two to four action words or one to three values. If additional nouns with deep significance come to you (like "Soul" did for me) or words from the "Who am I?" warm-up, add them to your Soul mission statement. Just try not to get mired in details or perfectionism.

This exercise may take some time and percolation to come to a statement that feels like "You." Just keep playing with it and give it space to develop. Feel free to revisit this exercise and continue to hone or tighten up your Soul mission statement.

CHAPTER 24

DISCERNING GOLDEN BREADCRUMBS

"Every time you don't follow your inner guidance, you feel a loss of energy, loss of power, a sense of spiritual deadness."
—SHAKTI GAWAIN

"Everybody is a genius. But if you judge a fish by its ability to climb a tree, it will live its whole life believing that it is stupid."
—ALBERT EINSTEIN

"Each person enters the world called."
—JAMES HILLMAN

A common encouragement comes from well-meaning adults as we are growing up: "You can do anything you put your mind to!" The theory subscribes to the idea that if we try hard enough, we can achieve whatever career or hobby we desire. This gives us endless opportunities and options. I disagree with this basic philosophy. Sure, if you try hard enough, you can get better at almost anything. But this is not the methodology of someone living a life aligned with their Soul. If we are allowing our lives to be led and orchestrated by the Soul, life becomes more about shedding instead of accomplishing, surrendering instead of achieving. We learn to let go of outer influences and options that are not truly authentic so we can open to the life that is meant for us.

Instead of looking at all the potential options, focus inward on the origin of your Self. The founder of archetypal psychology, James Hillman, introduces the "Acorn Theory" in his book *The Soul's Code: In Search of Character and Calling.* Hillman's theory, derived from Plato, is that we all have an inner daimon, or Soul guide, pulling us toward our unique greatness. As an acorn holds the entire pattern for a magnificent grown oak tree in its small, compact shell, we also have the blueprint from our Souls contained within each of us, guiding and calling to us. When fully actualized, we can look back and see the clues along the way where life and Soul were conspiring to bring us to our greatest Self. Instead of only viewing us as nature (biological/hormonal) or nurture (upbringing, family programming), we are subject to a third formless ingredient: the Soul.[24]

Like the legendary Brothers Grimm story of Hansel and Gretel, where the children leave breadcrumbs along the forest trail to find their way home, the Soul also leaves clues for us to find our way home. Golden breadcrumbs are the clues within our lives, composed of our unique skills, passions, and amazing synchronicities, that all conspire to show us our unique genius and our most powerful way to serve the planet. Instead of pushing a life agenda, we must begin to search for these inner clues. These crumbs, the clues to our true Selves, are not always found by our rational minds, but through the long, slow simmering of our unconscious intuitions. In order to find them, we need to have discernment about what is calling us toward a fuller, more alive expression of ourselves and what is only a distraction.

Often these distractions are seemingly intelligent, appealing, and smart moves that will bring us money, approval, or safety. When clients are in this stage of the hunt, I often put them on an "information diet." This is when it is crucial to limit our TV or Internet exposure, or even our exposure to opinionated friends or family members who take us away from discovering our own gold. We set boundaries to turn down the outer noise in order to get close to our own instincts, natural desires, and true feelings. We do this as long as we are vulnerable to forgetting *why* we are hunting for our golden breadcrumbs in the first place. After we have found several nuggets, we begin to believe and understand that there will be more, and we can relax a bit. It is through the experience on the path that wisdom is gained.

Wisdom is the resulting marriage of hard-won, real-life experiences and Soul orientation. Embodied wisdom is developed when we shed outer influences and become internally guided by the North Star of our genius. We recognize others when they are the holders of this type of energy. They feel grounded, centered, fully themselves, comfortable in their own skin—even with extreme character quirks and eccentricities.

It often feels to me as though these people have somehow managed to beat the system. They have escaped through a hidden trapdoor in the matrix. They are able to express the fullness of their inner fire while others around them have dimmed their flames. They do not ask permission to glow and are rewarded by the stoking passion from their work. They are focused and protected by the light of their higher, vaster selves. They have allowed themselves to hear and follow their Souls' marching orders, and, in turn, their lives have become enlivened.

Sometimes marching down the Soul's Path takes great courage. It can be very challenging when friends and family misunderstand or disapprove of the direction in which your Soul leads. The Soul's Path is not straight and orderly; it's winding and often bumpy, but it has an incredible view. While our ego doesn't understand why we're taking this confusing path, our Souls have an agenda, and all the detours are a necessary part of the bigger plan.

When we haven't seen the results from our Soul Work, we begin to compare ourselves with others: "All my friends seem to be happily married with children; why am I holed up in this apartment torturing myself day after day with this dumb book I'm trying to write?" Comparing yourself with others at this time is poison. When I worked in rehabs and with Alcoholics Anonymous, there was a common saying: "Never compare your insides with someone else's outsides."

On the spiritual path, we are frequently confronted by a teacher or program that claims to be able to answer all our pesky Soul questions. If we sign up for his newsletter, we will receive the five easy steps to eternal happiness. There is often a set formula or plan, and a clear answer for every question. You are signing up to join a paradigm—someone else's well-thought-out, or discovered, reality. You might be truly inspired, clearly witnessing their Soul plan in action, so the power and excitement jumping out of the computer screen may be very real. They might be on *their* Soul Path and so the energy is palpable around their connection with the Truth. It can be especially confusing when we, ourselves, are deep in the messiness of our own Soul Path. It is often at that crucial moment during an unfolding Soul project that we most need to trust in the dark. Yet the ego often interprets this essential part of the developmental process as complete torture and suffering. I equate this moment to the "transition" phase of birth labor. It is the moment right before the baby arrives when the laboring woman announces, "I can't do this! Cut it out of me! I'm dying!" It is in this crucial time that *five easy steps* sounds like a much-needed relief. That teacher/program appears to have all the kinks ironed out, wrapped up in a savvy marketing plan, while we're over here disheveled, cold, and muddy, alone in the dark, attempting to find yet another golden breadcrumb.

It is common to look outside yourself for answers, especially when feeling desperate. This is why it is crucial to build the muscle of listening to your own inner authority. Your business is to continually check in: "Does this idea, this intuition, feel like it is in alignment with the deepest part of myself? Does this feel like my most authentic me? Does it feel like the idea is trying to grab my attention and use my Self to serve in the world?" The challenging part of these questions is identifying part of yourself you haven't met yet. This is the unborn part of yourself, striving and struggling to be born while fighting for Her first breath.

It can be a bit of a mystery to put together the clues. I advise clients to find a special notebook in which to track all of their precious golden breadcrumbs. It can be extremely helpful during this fragile and flimsy period to have this physical space to cocoon the incubation of your Soul's dreams. Inspired daydreams, prophetic night dreams, books/workshops/movies/places, or stories that resonate with the deepest part of you can all be catalogued in this notebook for future validation, confirmation, and guidance.

As you are on your hunt in the dark woods for your golden breadcrumbs, remember they are discovered by what lights you up, what makes you feel most alive, and what you find to be beautiful. The clues pointing to your unique genius are the things that you are fascinated or even obsessed with. Even your "bad habits" are fertile ground to examine where Soul is trying to make Her presence felt.

When I was growing up, my mother, a mathematician herself, was always very concerned with my poor math skills. Instead of doing my painfully horrific math homework, I wanted to talk on the phone with my friends for hours upon hours. My parents thought this was an absolute waste of time; I should have been studying. They were worried that I was going to ruin my academic potential with all my socializing. This was a frequently heated debate topic around our household.

The other day, I laughed out loud when I remembered the drama of that time period. And I smiled as I realized that instead of dodging life, I was spending my time practicing, learning, and developing my unique gift. I now get paid to talk to people on the phone during Soul sessions. Part of my socialization and training came from those hours in middle school learning about myself and others. I was on my path even then, without knowing it. You are, too.

You will laugh when, later down the road, you look in your breadcrumb notebook and see how the signs and clues were there all along. You are now doing the very thing that is composed of the mosaic of your breadcrumbs. In the words of Oscar Wilde, "Be yourself; everyone else is already taken."

Soul Scavenger Hunt: Finding Golden Breadcrumbs

In your journal, write "Golden Breadcrumbs" on the top of a few pages. This is your safe place to list all the things that light you up, the things that you are drawn to. Think about the books, people, role models, movies, and so on that have captured your imagination for some reason. What are the golden breadcrumbs your Soul has laid for you on the trail of life? What are your passions, your hopes, your natural talents, your dreams, or the things that inspire you?

If you feel lost answering these questions, one good way to start is to think back to what you loved when you were young. Animals? Dance? Stand-up comedy? Puzzles? What things have naturally come easy to you? Maybe things others have commented on. Were there any amazing synchronicities, or meaningful coincidences, that occurred to help shed light on your unique mission? What would you enjoy doing now, even if you were not paid to do it? What is it you feel you most want to express or contribute to the planet? Describe your most fulfilling, enjoyable day. What happened?

You may also ask your Soul directly about where She thrives and what breadcrumbs She has laid out for you. Make a list of at least five of these golden breadcrumbs.

Poison of Comparison

Remember that comparing yourself with others can only inhibit you in your quest to find your Soul's mission. In your journal, write about how you interact with comparison. Are there any people whom you frequently compare yourself with? Is there someone's life that always looks more appealing than your own? Have a dialogue with your Soul and ask Her opinion. What does She think and want you to know about that person's role in your life? How does She feel when you compare yourself with him or her? Try to see your life from Her vantage point.

CHAPTER 25

THE BEAUTY WAY

"Beauty awakens the soul to act."
—DANTE ALIGHIERI

"Let us live for the beauty of our own reality."
—TOM ROBBINS

"Let the beauty of what you love be what you do."
—RUMI

Beauty often gets a bad rap. It is often classified as shallow, narcissistic, trivial, temporary, and fleeting. Yet, beauty is a Soul value. When we find something to be beautiful, we are overcome with the sacred desire to nourish and honor it. A beautiful altar in our home, a small corner of an overgrown garden, a Soul-nourishing meal—all of these things are crucial to the Soul. The Soul does not survive on concepts and ideas; the Soul drinks from the well of sensory nowness in physical form. Beauty invites us to join the eternal nature of the Soul with the temporary, changing, and constantly dying world of the physical. Beauty honors the uniquely feminine truth of the temporal world. Beauty calls us to be in intimate relationship with the shifting states of the earth. Whether that relationship is manifested through the care of the physical body, a physical space, or a cause that we deeply believe in, beauty leads our hearts to become more embodied and present.

Mother Teresa found service to be beautiful; Gandhi found peace to be beautiful; Martin Luther King, Jr., found equality to be beautiful. *Peace, service,* and *equality* are all invisible qualities, yet they are all also descriptors of beauty. These adjectives served as guides for these phenomenal leaders to live their lives in specific modes of devotion, in accordance with their Soul's values. We also can make beauty a priority in our lives—not as self-centered, but as Soul-centered.

When we make choices based on what we find to be beautiful, it becomes impossible to compare our lives with others'. Beauty activates feelings of devotion that encourage us to get out of our own egoic way and serve. The Soul is the part of us that finds things to be beautiful. This is why so many people speak of their Soul being touched through great art. Watching a Shakespearean play, marveling at the Sistine Chapel, or taking a walk in a beautifully landscaped park can all evoke intense gratitude for being a part of the mystery of humanity.

When we follow beauty we follow what feels alive, inspiring, nourishing, and compelling. One beauty pioneer I often think of is Martha Graham. Graham developed a style of modern dance that was ahead of her time by following her inner impulses of what she saw as beautiful. Frida Kahlo remained true to her authentic, honest style of what she found to be beautiful in life. Although her paintings often are based on painful topics like heartbreak and physical illness, they deeply resonate with many. Frida's authenticity has birthed legions of die-hard fans, and she is still one of the most sought-after and replicated artists today. These pioneers often fiercely follow beauty and choose their own authentic Truth over what is socially acceptable.

When we identify and follow what we believe to be beautiful in life, we are listening to our Souls. Of course, I am not talking about externally programmed beauty, which advertising commonly pushes, comparing our bodies or lives with what is currently deemed "attractive." I am speaking of big, inspiring Soul beauty. It is important for you to identify what you find beautiful on a Soul level.

This may be sparked within you when you arrange flowers, advocate for the rights of children, spend time with a friend who is depressed, or paint a room a new, beautiful color. Instead of making decisions based on safety, security, or practicality, the Soul wants us to live our lives according to what we find to be most beautiful. When you follow your true (not programmed) nature and desires, the world benefits from the expression of your you-ness.

When we feel beauty, it is felt deep within our hearts. When we follow beauty, we follow our hearts. The heart is not only a physical organ; it is an incredibly wise guidance system that can be used to make powerful decisions in our lives—to take us further on our Soul Journey. Heart-knowing is an advanced form of intelligence, where through feelings (energetic, emotional, and somatic) located quite literally in the heart center, we receive guidance from our Souls to make life decisions. The heart is the home of our intuitive voice, the tuning fork of beauty, and the seed of the blueprint of our Soul.

This incredible form of intelligence is inherently different from head-knowing. When we feel feelings of appreciation, compassion, or gratitude, our hearts emit a lovingly trustable signal. Heart-knowing is not a discounting of the rational world but, instead, a prioritization of our feeling reality. We check in with our bodies when weighing decisions and note which option inspires us with more energy and which option feels draining to our life force. We begin to sense which option closes our hearts and which expands our hearts' joy.

The challenges that we and our planet currently face are directly attributable to this head–heart split. The planet is at critical mass because of this imbalance of perspective. As humans we have used up our period of unconscious and careless head-dominated imbalance. By choosing finances over the inherent worth, beauty, and sustainability of our planet, we have thrown nature off balance. Our planet, humanity, and Souls all root for this crucial and essential reunion between rational head and embodied knowing through the heart. We help balance the planet when we make choices from beauty and the heart.

I often speak to clients who find themselves at a crossroads, wondering which career path to take. They will commonly weigh the factors of the marketplace, their skills, their interests and time, and financial expenditure for the necessary education. While these are all crucial factors in choosing a career, what about also factoring beauty into the equation? What job, career, or calling do you find to be most beautiful? When we make beauty a prioritizing element, we partner with Soul as we inquire what form of beauty has chosen us. This is when careers become callings.

If the Soul is the compass of life, then beauty is our true north. The following exercises will help you to identify, prioritize, and honor beauty as a Soul value. If we live our lives making heart-based decisions, when our lives come to an end, we will realize we lived lives of beauty, intuition, and inspiration. Life lived from heart is filled with meaning, wonder, and grace.

Heart-Knowing

This meditation will help you to become intimate with the way your heart speaks to you. (A free guided audio version of this meditation is available at www.ElisaRomeo.com/MeetYourSoul.)

Breathe (page 60), ground (page 59), and center (page 34). Then bring your awareness to your heart center. Does your heart feel soft and open or rigid and closed? With each breath, imagine your heart softening. On the exhale, "blow out" any fear or defensiveness that you have been holding around your heart. Do this for as long as you feel your heart opening and relaxing.

Next, think of a question that you are trying to get clarity on. Weigh your options and notice, with each one, how your heart feels. Which option feels more expansive and energized from within your heart and which feels shut down and draining? It can help to place one hand directly on your chest to feel your heartbeat and as a way to stay focused. As you somatically connect, you come to discover the incredible intelligence of the heart.

The Beauty Way

Many of us were not taught to make our decisions based on what we find to be the most beautiful. In your journal, explore the following questions:

- Was beauty an idea that was valued in your family growing up?

- What are the ways of living that inspire you?

- What are the most beautiful things, relationships, and experiences that you value in your life currently?

Once you have become more familiar with your relationship to beauty, in your journal, list five things that you have always wanted to try that you find to be beautiful. Commit to doing one of these things in the next few months.

CHAPTER 26

SOUL SURRENDER

"Every blade of grass has its Angel
that bends over it and whispers, 'Grow, grow.'"
—THE TALMUD

"Amor Fati—'Love Your Fate,' which is in fact your life."
—FRIEDRICH NIETZSCHE

"I do not fear their soldiers; my way lies open. I was born for this."
—JOAN OF ARC

As we deepen our relationship with our Soul, we begin to live a Soul-surrendered life. Surrender may sound easy. Maybe even like the easiest thing we've ever done. All we need to do is let go, right? We may even have images of people we know who have "let go" and identify with surrender, yet they may be more in avoidance or angry reaction to the "system." They may not be surrendering but avoiding or dissociating. I am not advocating for checking out, running, or splitting from the body. The type of surrender I refer to requires embodiment, maturation, and integration. That can shape us into being more rooted and invested in the planet. It is often the most terrifying thing we will ever do. To truly let go and surrender, we have to look straight into the eye of our biggest fears and call their bluff. Soul Surrender requires true, heartfelt feeling and discernment.

The type of surrender required by the Soul compels us into life wish, which is quite literally into the wish of our life. This wish is the true trajectory of the hero/heroine journey. Soul Surrender brings us into alignment with the very energy that beats our hearts. This requires consistently, courageously, and completely giving ourselves to the creative energy that has formed our cells and structured our physical body. It is also the very energy that forms the pattern and structure of our psychic lives. Once we surrender, we can begin to know and fight for this life force energy that has created our unique selves in this incarnation—our Souls themselves.

When the ego finally surrenders and rests in the backseat, we learn to hear, follow, and trust our Soul's marching orders. As you lessen the resistance toward Her, you suddenly have more energy in which to serve Her. If you take the time and energy to acknowledge your Soul, you give Her permission to enter your life and bless it. The ego stops fighting and cooperatively looks to the Soul for the answers to all the questions of Life.

Following the Soul's marching orders can make us feel crazy, isolated, and delusional, as they are rarely convenient or rational. We often don't understand exactly how we will benefit or what we will gain by following them. Because the Soul speaks through the subtle world of visuals, feelings, and dreams, She is often easy to initially write off and disregard. I say initially because She will always eventually make Her will known.

She first calls to us as a whisper (an inner nudge or feeling), then a clear statement (synchronicities, stronger feelings), and then, if we are still lacking the courage to heed Her call, she ups the ante with a fierce roar to get our attention (illness, crisis like the loss of a job or an accident). Again, this is not done out of punishment; it is from Her deep Love for us and her desire for us to "get the memo" in our lifetime.

It is not a lack of intuition that keeps us from listening to our Soul. We often are quite equipped with the details and information from our Soul that She has been hinting at. We have the proof of the somatic bodily reactions from avoiding Her call:

stomachaches, headaches, ulcers, and so on. We have the information that we know will lead us to our Soul. The issue is that we lack courage.

When we surrender to the Soul, we reanimate our sacred inner life. We build spiritual self-confidence when we choose to follow Her guidance. We learn to bow to Her and begin to give Her the reverence She deserves. Then we become worthy of our seat on the throne of our inner queendom (or kingdom). It is pure devotion that consistently, unwaveringly moves us from control to Soul. What we truly want is the freedom that comes from our commitment, dedication, and service to Her.

Moving from control to Soul is often terrifying. It might sound romantic, spiritual, or enlightened, but to trust the Soul is often terrifying to our identity. Who we think we are dies in order for us to realize our Soul's potential.

MORE DYING, LESS TRYING

The psychological and spiritual dying we must go through warrants the same respect, reverence, and honoring as any physical death. This dying is not for the faint of heart but is absolutely spiritually necessary. What is dying is old, outdated, control-oriented ways of approaching life: habits, beliefs, or goals that are no longer in alignment with the life your Soul wants for you.

When I was going through an intense period of "ego death," I would find myself neurotically spinning out, or ruminating. I would spend valuable energy questioning and analyzing things that were actually ready to die. This spiritual resistance is a part of the developmental process that occurs when our egos are being moved from the driver's seat to the backseat.

Whenever we surrender the ego's plan for the Soul's agenda, we experience a small piece of ego-death.

I remember one crucial night of spiritual discovery when I was crying on the floor, biting a towel, screaming, and swearing at the intense agony resulting from the persona and identity that I was leaving. I could feel the intense battle raging inside me between who I had always identified myself to be and the fear and promise of something new forming.

Soul Surrender occurs by discovering the Love of your fate, also known as *Amor Fati*. Love of one's fate is the panacea to spiritual dissociation. We fall so in love with our life wish that we become fully present and incarnated, committed to our lives on this planet. We start to listen to what our fullness is whispering to us and become curious about even the unpleasant, uncomfortable, and often time-consuming happenings of our daily lives. We begin to see the meaning and opportunity in deeply abusive relationships with family members or the irrational ex-lover whom we blamed for holding us energetically hostage.

Amor Fati means that we know we can pierce through our egos to our Souls and follow that guidance. We have accessed a part of ourselves that lies outside differing systems or others' interpretations. It does not matter if others understand. The only thing that matters is our relationship to Her. We begin to feel a sense of safety in the world because we understand our unique places in the universe. We can feel the interconnected web around us and see the reality of how synchronicities are golden breadcrumbs from the universe, reminding us that life is more than our stresses. There is an old saying that claims that we should all make time in our day that the "devil can't touch." Those moments of self-questioning, confusion, and lost wandering begin to shorten as moments with our Souls increase.

Your individual Soul Truth is trying to reach out and grab you at every moment, every day. And as much as I believe that not one Truth is right for everyone, I believe there *is* one Truth that is right for you, and that Truth is nonnegotiable. You do not need to be "special" or "evolved" to hear your Truth. You just need to have the courage and make the choice that you want to hear it more than you want to hear anything else. Think of it as Divine prioritizing.

More Dying, Less Trying Practice

In your journal, ponder the following questions: What needs to die in my life in order for my Soul to thrive? Are there things I need to release in order to hear and follow my Soul's marching orders?

Funeral Ritual

We often ruminate because we have not fully grieved something that has already died. Whether it is a job, relationship, opportunity, or health issue, if we find ourselves caught in mental loops, it may be a sign that we are distracting ourselves from feeling the deep pain that wants to be acknowledged. Creating a ritual gives us space to process our feelings and finally recognize that the old thing, belief, attitude, or plan has died.

One way I recommend to clients to do this is to plan your own funeral ritual for that part of you that must die. It is important to honor the death by taking it seriously and solemnly. Wear black, play some sad music, and allow yourself to weep. Write about how you are feeling and allow yourself to wallow. You may need to act, dance, or paint it out. Maybe you want it to be witnessed by a friend, or it may feel more appropriate to do it solo. Water is often cleansing, and it can feel like a rebirth to jump in a lake or ceremoniously leave your pain in the ocean. Fire is another important element representing transformation. A powerful ritual is to burn something symbolic like a letter or T-shirt from an old lover. Watch the ashes and smoke rise to the heavens as you release the old attachment.

CHAPTER 27

IT'S ALL GO(O)D

"What I am really saying is that you don't need to do anything, because if you see yourself in the correct way, you are all as much extraordinary phenomena of nature as trees, clouds, the patterns in running water, the flickering of fire, the arrangement of the stars, and the form of a galaxy. You are all just like that, and there is nothing wrong with you at all."
—ALAN WATTS

*"Only two things will remain with us across the river:
our inhering genius and the hearts we love.
In other words, what we do and whom we do it for."*
—STEVEN PRESSFIELD

"Many people are alive but don't touch the miracle of being alive."
—THICH NHAT HANH

Congratulations! You've made it to the final chapter. You have persisted through the intense unfolding of your Soul Journey and are ready for the final unveiling. We are now ready to clarify the incredible cosmic loophole in all this energetic battling for authenticity. Jesus knew it. Buddha felt it. Mary Magdalene embodied it. All great saints worshipped at the altar of this Truth behind all the other Truths: at the end of the day, the secret to all the battles, the simple clarity that arms you to become a Jedi warrior of Love, is understanding that it is *all* Good . . . it is *all* God.

Hold up! Remember, I use the term *God* not in an authoritarian way as a literalized entity. I am not talking about religion here. God is an energy. We can (and do) call it by many names: the great Creator, the universal Hum, the tenacious and determined flow of Life, the cosmic push toward cohesion, or even the interplanetary dance of grace.

We are gifted with the experience of being conscious and individual. This fantastic setup gives us the opportunity to reflect, witness, and interpret. With this gift comes responsibility. We have the free will to choose, in each and every moment, if God/the Creator/Life will witness itself through the unique and purposeful lens of our Souls.

Your individuated God Pod, your particular raindrop of consciousness, your interpretation of this Divine moment, is here now, joining this cosmic parade of destiny. Your participation is crucial in the overall story of creation. We are all *here:* sent (sometimes it feels more like trapped) but grounded and physically present within the bounds of our individual natures to shine as one incredible, unmistakable thread in the weaving of this incredible mythic tale. It is through your individual Soul nature that you bless the cosmic creator that has partnered with your Soul to give you life.

When you surrender to your Soul, you surrender to God. You participate, consciously, in the most delicious merging available between the physical and the spiritual worlds. Your life becomes art in service of Love as you honor and listen to the voice of your deepest instincts, beauty, and joy. To embody Soul on Earth is absolutely no easy task; it is never "done" or "finished." A test always exists, and we are often left alone for validation from only our Souls. As long as we are participants in the physical world, we have front row seats to the "Maya Magic Show." Bound by the material and sensory world, we are prone to fall for her illusory sleight of hand and lose our spiritual vision.

Can you stare directly at evil and find the God/Good? Can you witness torture, pain, misery, injustice, and brutal violence and find where Love is masking itself? Even in the darkest face of evil there exists a pulse of Love. Can we be, like Jesus, so Love-stubborn that we refuse to minimize our perspective to only the physical world? Can we find the God/Good in every moment so that it is amplified and glorified?

We are called here to Love. Love calls us to be more, to enter wholeheartedly into life. Your mission, should you choose to accept it, is to love your Self, your Soul, like God loves your Soul. Then you understand and feel the clarity and purpose in which you were perfectly and specifically designed. When you surrender to your purpose, you accept your mission: to get out of the way and serve your unique path of Love. Soul Love is never narcissistic; it is the Love of the Divine showing up as our individual face of God.

The core of the life wish is eternal Soul Love. Love does not seek reaction, cling to expectation, or fear disappointment. Love is not concerned with the ego's understanding of physical reality. The true energy of Love confidently and unwaveringly burns away all sediment that clings to story while dropping us into the naked and raw hum of right now. The guidance of Love is direct and always married to Presence. It is not concerned with granting wants or wishes, but offers what is truly needed on a Soul level in the moment—all while being accompanied by an exhilarating feeling of vibrant aliveness.

When we die, we don't take our cars or clothes or 401(k). What we do take is Love and consciousness, which are the accumulation of embodied experience, hard lessons learned, and joy. The core of the heart beats with the desire to be known. Not to be known, recognized, and understood by the external world, but a knowing of and by the separated self in the whole and certain reality of the unseparated one. The Soul lovingly longs for this reunion—this cosmic homecoming—to welcome the weary ego back into the loving reverberation of the whole being. When this homecoming occurs, the ego's micromanagement of the Divine and the lived understanding that the universe is all a result of random chance or interesting scientific fact is demolished. The experience of sheer grace is excruciating to the ego, and the unwavering and pulsing Love that lives behind the veil of this earthy hologram dismembers any remaining beliefs in the haphazard-ness behind the "what is" of any moment. The internal and external have joined to become one fluid dance yet again. The dancer becomes the dancing in this alchemical process of above–below, within–without. The awareness shifts the unnerving and unsatisfied mantra of the mind from "Is this real?" to a deep and humble bow from the ego to the Divinity of the God Self. In order for this metaphorical bow to be a successful gesture in which this psychospiritual process can occur, the mind must be fully at rest and in contact with the floor, where it is finally no longer higher than the value of the heart. The surrendered state of the God Self has now occurred as the heart takes its natural position as the center—not only of the physical body but of all decisions.

Consider this your "get out of jail free" card: we are incredibly blessed because of our inherent and organic link to eternal Soul. Soul remembering and recognition are the links to realizing our paths through the dark to return to our original source of Love.

The Soul Journey is about giving birth to your true Self. This is your most authentic and loving face of God, the desperately needed Soul. If you can get very quiet, with deep humility and reverence, and earnestly ask your Soul, "What are your intentions for my life? What will you have me be?" you will receive your answer. The world waits in Love for your reply.

RESOURCES

PART I: UNDERSTANDING THE SOUL

Chapter 1: Be Soul-Centered

The following books on Soul may have slightly different definitions of Soul from my own, but I have found meaning and resonance with these Soul authors.

- *Care of the Soul: A Guide for Cultivating Depth and Sacredness in Everyday Life,* by Thomas Moore (New York: HarperPerennial, 1994)

- *The Seat of the Soul,* by Gary Zukav (New York: Fireside, 1999)

- *Your Soul's Plan: Discovering the Real Meaning of the Life You Planned Before You Were Born,* by Robert Schwartz (Berkeley: Frog Books, 2009)

Chapter 2: The Spirit and the Soul

Amma: An incredible example of a Divine feminine Soul in the world is the spiritual teacher and "hugging saint" Amma, an embodied and powerful activist for the planet. Check out her work and see how you can help: www.amma.org.

Angela Farmer: Many speak of the feminine, but few are

actually running the energy throughout their bodies. Yogi Angela Farmer is an incredible example of embodied feminine energy, and we are lucky to have her teachings available to us. Yoga like you've never experienced it! Both of her DVDs are available via her website: www.angela-victor.com.

- *The Feminine Unfolding: An Exploration of Yoga with Angela Farmer* [DVD], Claudia Cummins (director), Angela-Victor, 1999

- *Inner Body Flow* [DVD], Angela Farmer (director), 2005

Books:

- *Conscious Femininity: Interviews with Marion Woodman,* by Marion Woodman (Toronto: Inner City Books, 1993)

- *Emptiness Dancing,* by Adyashanti (Boulder, CO: Sounds True, 2006)

Chapter 3: The Ego and the Soul

Stanislav Grof: Stanislav Grof, one of my inspiring professors from Pacifica Graduate Institute, is known as the founder of Transpersonal Psychology. His Holotropic Breathwork is a powerful way to open the ego to Soul experiences: www.holotropic.com.

- *Spiritual Emergency: When Personal Transformation Becomes a Crisis (New Consciousness Readers),* by Stanislav Grof and Christina Grof (New York: Tarcher, 1989)

Spiritual Emergence (Canada): Spiritualemergence.net (out of Canada) is a hotline for individuals having psycho-spiritual or transformative crises. Contact them by phone at 604-533-3545 or by e-mail at spiritual.emergence@shaw.ca. An important service for individuals having spiritual emergency issues, the hotline is staffed by skilled volunteers and is a great cause to which to donate.

Spiritual Emergence (U.S.): The Spiritual Emergence Network has referrals for therapists trained in dealing with spiritual emergency: www.spiritualemergence.info.

Chapter 4: Life Versus Death Wish

Books:

- *Love Is Letting Go of Fear,* by Gerald G. Jampolsky (Berkeley: Celestial Arts, 2004)

- *The Luxury of Afterwards: The Christine Downing Lectures at San Diego State University 1995–2004,* by Christine Downing (Lincoln, NE: iUniverse, 2004)

PART II: MEETING YOUR SOUL

Chapter 5: Have Some Humble Pie

Andrew Harvey: If anyone can help to humble the ego next to the power of the invisibles, it's Andrew Harvey. After an interview with him, I felt the power of his Love for the Divine resonating throughout my body for weeks. To learn more, check out *Radical Passion: Sacred Love and Wisdom in Action,* by Andrew Harvey (Berkeley: North Atlantic Books, 2012).

Chapter 6: The Power of Prayer

Books:

- *Invisible Acts of Power: Channeling Grace in Your Everyday Life,* by Caroline Myss (New York: Atria Books, 2006)

- *Light the Flame: 365 Days of Prayer,* by Andrew Harvey (Carlsbad, CA: Hay House, 2013)

Chapter 7: Seeing the Invisibles

Psychic Horizons Meditation School: I highly recommend the meditation and clairvoyant training program I attended, if you are in or around the San Francisco Bay Area: Psychic Horizons Meditation School in San Francisco, www.psychichorizons.com.

Wake Up: I also highly recommend the relatable, amusing, and grounded documentary *Wake Up*. In it, Jonas Elrod is living his life when a good friend dies in a motorcycle accident. The result is a spiritual opening where he begins to see energies and spirits. The story follows him and his girlfriend, Mara, as he navigates modern medicine, psychology, and current spiritual teachers and practices. Watch his courageous spiritual development. Check out this film, directed by Jonas Elrod and Chloe Crespi, produced by Steve Hutensky (2010); DVD produced by Walk the Walk Entertainment and Open Eye Productions and distributed by Beyond Words Publishing (2010). Learn more at www.wakeupthefilm.com.

Books:

- *Energy Anatomy: The Science of Personal Power, Spirituality, and Health,* by Caroline Myss (Boulder, CO: Sounds True, 2001)

- *Hands of Light: A Guide to Healing Through the Human Energy Field*, by Barbara Brennan, illustrated by Jos. A. Smith (New York: Bantam, 1988)

- *The Secret of the Soul: Using Out-of-Body Experiences to Understand Our True Nature,* by William Buhlman (New York: HarperCollins, 2001)

Chapter 8: Meditation

Binaural Beats: Binaural beats (subliminal rhythms, undetectable consciously) can be helpful to raise your brain state during meditation. There are many different styles, but one CD I recommend is *Theta Meditation System,* by Dr. Jeffrey Thompson (Boulder, CO: Sounds True, 2001).

Guided Meditation: Meditation can often be overwhelming in the beginning. Learning to silence the mind and relax can be shocking when we are used to a busy mind. A great place to begin is with a guided meditation. On my website, www.ElisaRomeo.com, there are free guided audios available for this book and others for purchase, such as the extended "Meet Your Soul" meditation.

Books:

- *Falling into Grace: Insights on the End of Suffering,* by Adyashanti (Boulder, CO: Sounds True, 2013)

- *Getting in the Gap: Making Conscious Contact with God Through Meditation* (Book & CD), by Dr. Wayne W. Dyer (Carlsbad, CA: Hay House, 2002)

- *The Breathing Book: Good Health and Vitality Through Essential Breath Work,* by Donna Farhi (New York: Henry Holt and Co., 1996)

- *Wherever You Go, There You Are: Mindfulness Meditation in Everyday Life,* by Jon Kabat-Zinn (New York: Hyperion, 1995)

Chapter 9: The Soul Speaks: Soul Journaling

Book:

- *Leaving My Father's House: A Journey to Conscious Femininity,* by Marion Woodman with Kate Danson, Mary Hamilton, and Rita Greer Allen (Boston: Shambhala Publications, 1992)

PART III: MOVING THROUGH THE BLOCKS

Chapter 10: Soul Orchestration

Emily Kellow Graham: After losing her baby daughter to Trisomy 18, Emily Kellow Graham has helped educate and shift policies at hospitals for women receiving similar devastating news. She creates bereavement packets for families to receive and is working on a children's book for the kids of families in these situations. Learn more at www.norainourfamily.org.

Dark Nights: The books below can help you understand the dark night of the soul. For additional resources focused on Spiritual Emergency, see "The Ego and the Soul" (Chapter 3).

- *Dark Night of the Soul,* by St. John of the Cross, translated by Mirabai Starr, foreword by Thomas Moore (New York: Riverhead Trade, 2003)

- *Dark Nights of the Soul: A Guide to Finding Your Way Through Life's Ordeals,* by Thomas Moore (New York: Gotham, 2005)

- *Man's Search for Meaning,* by Viktor E. Frankl (Boston: Beacon Press, 2006)

- *Spiritual Madness: The Necessity of Meeting God in Darkness,* by Caroline Myss (Boulder, CO: Sounds True, 2002)

- *When Things Fall Apart: Heart Advice for Difficult Times,* by Pema Chodron (Boston: Shambhala Publications, 2000)

Suicide Help: If you feel suicidal, call the National Suicide Prevention Lifeline at 1-800-273-TALK. (You can also search their website, by state, to find the crisis center in your area: www.suicidepreventionlifeline.org.) Please do not be afraid to reach out and call. At the first suicide line I worked at, one of our best clinicians was a man who had called the center himself at a dark time and went on to become an incredible clinician and very happy man. Hang on and reach out for help. It WILL get better.

Book:

- *The Soul's Code: In Search of Character and Calling,* by James Hillman (New York: Random House, 1997)

Chapter 11: Burden of Proof

Gary Schwartz: I heard Gary Schwartz speak when I was attending the University of Washington. I was impressed by his research and Soul mission to bridge science with the paranormal. Two books of his that I found extremely helpful are:

- *The Afterlife Experiments: Breakthrough Scientific Evidence of Life after Death,* by Gary E. Schwartz (New York: Atria Books, 2003)

- *The Sacred Promise: How Science Is Discovering Spirit's Collaboration with Us in Our Daily Lives,* by Gary E. Schwartz (New York: Atria Books, 2011)

Michael Talbot: The following Michael Talbot books do a great job of stretching our stuck thinking around what is and what is not possible.

- *Beyond the Quantum,* by Michael Talbot (New York: Bantam, 1988)

- *The Holographic Universe: The Revolutionary Theory of Reality,* by Michael Talbot (New York: HarperPerennial, 2011)

- *Mysticism and the New Physics,* by Michael Talbot (London: Penguin Books/Compass, 1993)

Near Death Experience Research Foundation: A website (www.nderf.org) that compiles individuals' accounts of their near-death experiences. It is easy to spend many hours reading all the incredible accounts. This is where I first discovered Anita Moorjani's incredible account. Anita was dying from cancer, with her organs shutting down, when she had an incredible near-death experience that healed her cancer and gave her life new meaning.

- *Dying to Be Me: My Journey from Cancer, to Near Death, to True Healing,* by Anita Moorjani (Carlsbad, CA: Hay House, 2012)

Richard Tarnas: A professor I studied with at Pacifica Graduate Institute, Richard Tarnas is an impeccable mind with incredible Soul. His book covers the Copernican Shift, giving context as to why, in modern society, we have become disenchanted and have such trouble accepting the natural world of the Soul.

- *The Passion of the Western Mind: Understanding the Ideas That Have Shaped Our World View,* by Richard Tarnas (New York: Ballantine Books, 1993)

Books:

- *Entangled Minds: Extrasensory Experiences in a Quantum Reality,* by Dean Radin (New York: Paraview Pocket Books, 2006)

- *Extraordinary Knowing: Science, Skepticism, and the Inexplicable Powers of the Human Mind,* by Elizabeth Lloyd Mayer (New York: Bantam, 2007)

- *When the Impossible Happens: Adventures in Non-Ordinary Reality,* by Stanislav Grof (Boulder, CO: Sounds True, 2005)

- *The Divine Matrix: Bridging Time, Space, Miracles, and Belief,* by Gregg Braden (Carlsbad, CA: Hay House, 2008)

Chapter 12: Soul-nesia

The Velveteen Rabbit: Not just for children—this story is a classic about what is "Real": *The Velveteen Rabbit,* by Margery Williams, illustrated by William Nicholson (New York: Doubleday, 1958)

Chapter 13: Fool's Gold

Books:

- *A Holy Life: The Writings of St. Bernadette of Lourdes,* by Patricia McEachern (San Francisco, CA: Ignatius Press, 2005)

- *Jung and Tarot: An Archetypal Journey,* by Sallie Nichols (York Beach, ME: Weiser Books, 1980)

Chapter 14: Fear Gremlins

Books:

- *A Master Class in Gremlin-Taming: The Absolutely Indispensable Next Step for Freeing Yourself from the Monster of the Mind,* by Rick Carson (New York: William Morrow Paperbacks, 2008)

- *Taming Your Gremlin: A Surprisingly Simple Method for Getting Out of Your Own Way,* by Rick Carson (New York: Quill, 2003)

Chapter 15: The Enemy Is a Good Teacher

Book:

- *The Art of Happiness (Tenth Anniversary Edition): A Handbook for Living,* by Dalai Lama (New York: Riverhead Books, 2009)

Chapter 16: Divine Shit Storms

Books:

- *Listening to the Oracle: The Ancient Art of Finding Guidance in the Signs and Symbols All Around Us,* by Dianne Skafte, Ph.D. (San Francisco: HarperSanFrancisco, 1997)

- *Romancing the Shadow: A Guide to Soul Work for a Vital, Authentic Life,* by Connie Zweig and Steven Wolf (New York: Ballantine, 1999)

- *Owning Your Own Shadow: Understanding the Dark Side of the Psyche,* by Robert A. Johnson (San Francisco: HarperSanFrancisco, 2009)

Chapter 17: Checked Out with Trauma

For clinicians: For clinicians working with trauma, I recommend the Seeking Safety Program by Lisa M. Najavits, professor of psychiatry at Boston University School of Medicine. Using this program at several rehabs, I witnessed clients gain practical tools to give the ego a healthy and safe place outside the trauma story and learn to create healthy boundaries. I highly recommend this well-thought-out and respectful program, especially for clients with PTSD and substance issues. Learn more at www.seekingsafety.org or read *Seeking Safety: A Treatment Manual for PTSD and Substance Abuse,* by Lisa M. Najavits (New York: Guilford Press, 2002).

The Foundation for Shamanic Studies: www.shamanism.org.

Sandra Ingerman: Sandra Ingerman is a licensed therapist as well as a gifted shamanic practitioner. I recommend her work wholeheartedly. Learn more at www.sandraingerman.com.

- *Soul Retrieval: Mending the Fragmented Self,* by Sandra Ingerman (New York: HarperOne, 2006)

- *The Beginner's Guide to Shamanic Journeying,* by Sandra Ingerman (Boulder, CO: Sounds True, 2003)

Therapies:

- **EFT/Tapping:** Nick Ortner is a leader in the field of tapping. His website (www.thetappingsolution.com) has a nice intro video on how to start and information on how to find a practitioner in your area. His book is a great place to begin: *The Tapping Solution:*

A Revolutionary System for Stress-Free Living, by Nick Ortner (Carlsbad, CA: Hay House, 2013).

- **EMDR:** If you are experiencing more intense anxiety, crippling panic attacks, or PTSD, I recommend Eye Movement Desensitization and Reprocessing (EMDR). It was founded by Dr. Francine Shapiro, who, while walking in the park, noticed that eye movements appeared to decrease the negative emotions associated with her own stressful memories. EMDR has been shown to be very effective for trauma. To find a clinician, go to www.emdr.com or check out the EMDR International Association (EMDRIA) at www.emdria.org.

- **Shamanic Soul Retrieval:** I can personally recommend Michael Harner, author of the incredibly popular *The Way of the Shaman* (New York: HarperOne, 1990), having attended his shamanic training workshops. He has a wonderful website with information on his training programs as well as information on finding certified shamanic counselors: www.shamanism.org.

Books:

- *Coping with Trauma: Hope Through Understanding,* by Jon G. Allen (Arlington, VA: American Psychiatric Publishing, 2004)

- *Healing Trauma: A Pioneering Program for Restoring the Wisdom of Your Body,* by Peter A. Levine (Boulder, CO: Sounds True, 2006)

- *Waking the Tiger: Healing Trauma,* by Peter A. Levine (Berkeley: North Atlantic Books, 1997)

Chapter 18: Feeling Versus Emoting

Eugene Gendlin: Focusing is an incredible mind/body technique that reduces stress while building self-awareness and inner wisdom. Created by psychologist Eugene Gendlin, this technique has been popular since the 1980s. Learn more by reading *Focusing,* by Eugene T. Gendlin (New York: Bantam Books, 1982).

Chapter 19: Spiritual Temper Tantrums

Gratitude: One of the best antidotes for a spiritual temper tantrum is gratitude. The following guide will help you get your daily dose of "Vitamin G": *Living in Gratitude: Mastering the Art of Giving Thanks Every Day, A Month-by-Month Guide,* by Angeles Arrien (Boulder, CO: Sounds True, 2013).

Chapter 20: Spiraling Out

Understanding Types of Thought: This is a great workbook I have used for clients working on understanding the difference between black-and-white versus "rainbow" thinking, setting loving limits, and understanding the various stages of recovery: *The Don't Diet, Live-It! Workbook: Healing Food, Weight and Body Issues,* by Andrea Wachter and Marsea Marcus (Carlsbad, CA: Gurze Books, 1999).

Books:

- *Addiction to Perfection: The Still Unravished Bride: A Psychological Study (Studies in Jungian Psychology),* by Marion Woodman (Toronto: Inner City Books, 1982)

- *Women, Food, and God: An Unexpected Path to Almost Everything,* by Geneen Roth (New York: Scribner, 2011)

Chapter 21: Who's to Judge?

Energetic Codependency: My 2012 e-book, available via my website, covers the important topic of "energetic codependency." Energetic codependency is described as: "How I feel depends on how you feel." Clairsentient, empathic, sensitive people are especially at risk of losing themselves to this common issue. We learn why we lose our energy and how to set healthy energetic boundaries to stop getting drained by the energy of events or those around us: *Authentic Intuition,* by Elisa Romeo (available at www.ElisaRomeo.com).

Chapter 22: Who, Me? Claiming Spiritual Authority

Kumare: Filmmaker Vikram Gandhi creates a fake guru character and ends up building a real following. This is a great film that highlights the importance of preserving our spiritual authority. (Also fascinating to watch is how Vikram becomes victim to his own game—his "fake" character actually emits real spiritual wisdom and healing power from his Soul, beyond his own understanding, thereby transforming him.) Learn more at www.kumaremovie.com (director: Vikram Gandhi; production companies: Future Bliss Films, Disposable Television; Future Bliss Films distributor: Kino Lorber, 2012).

PART IV: CLAIMING YOUR SOUL LIFE

Chapter 23: So . . . What's My Purpose?

Elisa Romeo: My website is filled with tons of free information (articles and videos) to dive deep into discovering and living your Soul's purpose (www.ElisaRomeo.com).

Chapter 24: Discerning Golden Breadcrumbs

Books:

- *I Could Do Anything If I Only Knew What It Was: How to Discover What You Really Want and How to Get It,* by Barbara Sher (New York: Dell, 1995)

- *Live the Life You Love: In Ten Easy Step-by-Step Lessons,* by Barbara Sher (New York: Dell, 1997)

- *The Soul's Code: In Search of Character and Calling,* by James Hillman (New York: Random House, 1997)

- *Thomas Moore on Meaningful Work,* by Thomas Moore (Boulder, CO: Sounds True, 1997)

- *What Should I Do with My Life?: The True Story of People Who Answered the Ultimate Question,* by Po Bronson (New York: Ballantine Books, 2005)

Chapter 25: The Beauty Way

Books:

- *The Art of Extreme Self-Care: Transform Your Life One Month at a Time,* by Cheryl Richardson (Carlsbad, CA: Hay House, 2012)

- *When I Loved Myself Enough,* by Kim McMillen and Alison McMillen Sidgwick (London: Jackson, 2001)

- *You Can Heal Your Life* (Gift Edition), by Louise L. Hay (Carlsbad, CA: Hay House, 1999)

Chapter 26: Soul Surrender

Book:

- *The Ecstasy of Surrender: 12 Surprising Ways Letting Go Can Empower Your Life,* by Judith Orloff (New York: Harmony, 2014)

Chapter 27: It's All Go(o)d

Book:

- *The Book: On the Taboo Against Knowing Who You Are,* by Alan Watts (New York: Vintage Books, 1972)

NOTES

1. Marion Woodman, *Conscious Femininity: Interviews with Marion Woodman* (Toronto: Inner City Books, 1993), 18–19.

2. Ibid., 116.

3. Adyashanti, *Emptiness Dancing* (Boulder, CO: Sounds True, 2006), 147–148.

4. Christine Downing, *The Luxury of Afterwards: The Christine Downing Lectures at San Diego State University 1995–2004* (Lincoln, NE: iUniverse, 2004), 65.

5. *Reality Bites (Tenth Anniversary Edition),* directed by Ben Stiller (Los Angeles: Universal Studios, 1994).

6. Downing, *The Luxury of Afterwards,* 64.

7. Paula Reeves, *Women's Intuition: Unlocking the Wisdom of the Body* (Berkeley: Conari Press, 2011), 7–8.

8. S. B. Most et al., "How Not to Be Seen: The Contribution of Similarity and Selective Ignoring to Sustained Inattentional Blindness," *Psychological Science* 12, no. 1 (January 2001): 9–17.

9. Mihaly Csikszentmihalyi, *Flow: The Psychology of Optimal Experience* (New York: HarperPerennial, 1991).

10. John Welwood, *Toward a Psychology of Awakening: Buddhism, Psychotherapy, and the Path of Personal and Spiritual Transformation* (Boston: Shambhala Publications, 2002), 12.

11. Robert Augustus Masters, *Spiritual Bypassing: When Spirituality Disconnects Us from What Really Matters* (Berkeley: North Atlantic Books, 2010), 2.

12. "Evolutionary Mysticism" podcast with Andrew Harvey and Tami Simon, accessed July 15, 2014, www.soundstrue.com/podcast/transcripts/andrew-harvey.php?camefromhome=camefromhome.

13. Merriam-Webster Online, "Scientific Method," accessed July 15, 2014, www.merriam-webster.com/dictionary/scientific-method.

14. Edward Granville Brown, *A Literary History of Persia* (New York: Cambridge University Press, 2009), 299.

15. François Trochu, *St. Bernadette Soubirous: 1844–1879* (Charlotte, NC: TAN Books, 1957).

16. Rick Carson, *Taming Your Gremlin: A Surprisingly Simple Method for Getting Out of Your Own Way* (New York: Quill, 2003).

17. C. G. Jung, *Aion: Researches into the Phenomenology of the Self* (Princeton, NJ: Princeton University Press, 1979), 217.

18. M. E. Seligman and S. F. Maier, "Failure to Escape Traumatic Shock," *Journal of Experimental Psychology* 74, no. 1 (May 1967): 1–9.

19. Marion Woodman, *Addiction to Perfection: The Still Unravished Bride* (Toronto: Inner City Books, 1982), 32.

20. Ibid., 72.

21. Elisa Romeo, *Authentic Intuition: A Psychological and Energetic Guide to Find Your Purpose, Claim Your Life and Live with Joy* (e-book, 2012).

22. Caroline Myss, *Entering the Castle: Finding the Inner Path to God and Your Soul's Purpose* (New York: Free Press, 2007), 44.

23. *The Lego Movie,* directed by Phil Lord and Christopher Miller (Los Angeles: Warner Bros., 2014).

24. James Hillman, *The Soul's Code: In Search of Character and Calling* (New York: Random House, 1997).

INDEX OF EXERCISES

ACKNOWLEDGMENTS

I have been extremely blessed with many amazing supporters of my work and this book.

First off, thanks to my clients, who constantly inspire me. Your willingness to listen and follow Soul is humbling and beautiful to witness. Thank you for allowing me to be a part of your Soul Journeys.

Thank you also to the clients who shared their incredible stories and Soul journaling for the book. (You know I would love to shout your names from the rooftops!) My favorite parts of the book are feeling your individual Souls strongly come through onto the pages. Your courage and honesty will help others find and connect to their own inner knowing.

To Kasey Crown, a true Soul Sister, thank you for your unwavering integrity, vision, and heart. Your navigation of the spiritual world makes you not only a trusted clinician but a wonderful friend. You bless this world with your Presence.

To Jane Dobson House, thank you for your cosmic humor, your ability to fly masterfully between the realms, and your loyal friendship. I treasure our long talks that result in many of my "aha" moments.

To Pacifica Graduate Institute (faculty and classmates) for being a place where the sacred is held every day with the practical.

To Psychic Horizons, my meditation school, in San Francisco. Thank you for the top-notch instruction and impeccable ethics and for teaching me that spiritual work can be both serious and hilarious at the same time.

To my inspiring teachers whom I have been so deeply blessed to study with, work with, and learn from—my endless gratitude: Marion Woodman, Maureen Murdock, Dianne Skafte, Christine Downing, Stephen Aizenstat, Michael Conforti, Michael and Sandra Harner, Richard Tarnas, and Stanislav Grof.

To Tracy Dickerson for introducing me to the world of the invisibles. At a crucial time in my life, you were a dependable guide to help me see that there is so much more than only physical reality.

To Joanna Pyle, a true spiritual explorer. Your wisdom and heart are always exactly what is needed in the moment. Several years ago you looked at me and asked, "Where is your book?" I'm sure you weren't aware at the time, but that moment planted the seed that got me wondering the exact same thing.

To Cheryl Richardson for your intuitive persistence and fierce mojo during the Hay House writer's conference that caused me to cry in front of an audience, face my fears, and state who I *really* am out loud for the first time.

To Reid Tracy for sharing your precious time and wisdom (from years of pioneering and grounded experience). Thank you for following your Soul and being a true supporter of healing for the planet.

To Louise Hay. I first read *You Can Heal Your Life* cover to cover on the floor of a hospital gift shop. I was blown away by the amount of grace emanating from the book. Thank you for being an inspiring pioneer of Love.

To Heather Bruce Allison of Heather B. Allison Photography. Besides being the most incredible photographer, you are absolutely the most fun to get woo-woo with. Thank you for your artistic vision, psychic text messages, and long friendship.

To Jen Wasson of Wasson Design. How did I manage to find a best friend who is my all-time favorite designer? I am endlessly grateful for your patience and visionary eye. You brought the book cover, the illustrations, and my website all from my heart into the world, in a better version than I could ever have imagined.

To Emily and Alex Graham, along with the entire Kellow family. I have learned so much from you all! Emmy, I am endlessly humbled to call you a friend and experience your wisdom, fierce Love, and grace within my life.

Thank you to Claire Bidwell Smith for answering a Soul Prayer and encouraging me to send my manuscript to your talented agent. Your psychopomp navigation abilities, keen sense of observation, and grounded humor make you a triple threat.

To my dream team: Wendy Sherman, agent extraordinaire. You are a true literary matchmaker! I'm so thankful that I was brought to you and your keen intuition. To Patty Gift for following your gut on a brand-new author. I am so blessed to work with such a true talent who is dedicated to consciousness and kindness as well. Thank you endlessly to my editor at Hay House, Laura Gray. You blow my mind and are an amazing editor. Thank you for cleaning while keeping my voice intact and having the organizational skills that I was not born with! Working with you was wonderful, and you made this book shine.

Sharon Romeo, thank you endlessly for your constant and steady encouragement to write and get this book out into the world.

To my mother, Mary Romeo. Thank you a million times for all the incredible real-world support, from child care to bear hugs. This book would not have been possible without you. Thank you for raising me to question the world while also trusting it.

Thank you to my father, Nick Romeo, for incarnating as my opposing Sun and showing me that I Know everything I have ever truly needed to. Thank you for your delicious Italian meals, love, fathering, and always prioritizing your family as number one. We all miss you so much.

Thank you, Luca, for birthing me as I birth you and this book. I will never forget timing my contractions as I wrote the introduction. Your Soul has a great sense of humor already.

Thank you, Van, for inspiring me every day to stay present, slow down, and be awake. You teach me that life without joy is no life at all. I am so blessed to be your mama. I love you more than infinity + one.

And to my spiritual teacher and beloved, Adam Foley. This book would not *be* without you. The mirror of your Soul is the most incredible, inspiring form of beauty I have ever known. Thank you for loving Sophia, fighting for Her, and seeing Her when I cannot. Thank you for wanting my freedom, often more consciously than even I do. You are everything that is beautiful to me. I am Love for You.

ABOUT THE AUTHOR

Elisa Romeo, M.A., M.F.T., is a psychic medium, a licensed marriage and family therapist, an author, and a speaker. Her worldwide private practice, which grew by word of mouth, consists of thousands of clients, whom she works with by merging a background in depth psychology with an ability to directly communicate with the Soul. Elisa knows that not only do we all have a purpose but we each hold within us powerful Divine potential that calls out for fulfillment. She believes that each of us has amazing psychic abilities, immense healing potential, and spiritual gifts, which many of us have long forgotten. Her mission is to help us connect to our unique Soul Voice so we can hear Her guidance, power, and Love. Elisa is known for speaking the language of the Soul with humility, humor, and grounded candor. Learn more at www.ElisaRomeo.com.

Hay House Titles of Related Interest

YOU CAN HEAL YOUR LIFE, the movie, starring Louise Hay & Friends
(available as a 1-DVD program and an expanded 2-DVD set)
Watch the trailer at: www.LouiseHayMovie.com

THE SHIFT, the movie, starring Dr. Wayne W. Dyer
(available as a 1-DVD program and an expanded 2-DVD set)
Watch the trailer at: www.DyerMovie.com

* * *

DEFY GRAVITY: Healing Beyond the Bounds of Reason, by Caroline Myss

DYING TO BE ME: My Journey from Cancer, to Near Death, to True Healing, by Anita
Moorjani

FOR LOVERS OF GOD EVERYWHERE: Poems of the Christian Mystics,
by Roger Housden

THE HOPE: A Guide to Sacred Activism, by Andrew Harvey

THE POWER OF INTENTION, by Dr. Wayne W. Dyer

WRITING IN THE SAND: Jesus, Spirituality, and the Soul of the Gospels,
by Thomas Moore

YOU CAN HEAL YOUR LIFE, by Louise Hay

All of the above are available at your local bookstore,
or may be ordered by contacting Hay House (see next page).

* * *